EXODUS

EXODUS

Let My People Go

Daniel Berrigan

with a foreword by
Ched Myers

CASCADE *Books* · Eugene, Oregon

EXODUS
Let My People Go

Cascade Books
A Division of Wipf and Stock Publishers
199 W. 8th Ave., Suite 3
Eugene, OR 97401

ISBN: 978-1-55635-105-1

Cataloging-in-Publication data:

Berrigan, Daniel.

    Exodus : Let my people go / Daniel Berrigan. With a foreword by Ched Myers.

    xiv + 168 p. ; 23 cm.

    ISBN: 978-1-55635-105-1

    1. Bible. O.T. Exodus—Commentaries. I. Myers, Ched. II. Title.

BS1245. 53 .B47 2008

Manufactured in the U.S.A.

Whither bound
we know not.
And yet
we know.

Contents

Foreword

The first time I heard Daniel Berrigan speak was early in 1976 at the Newman Center in Berkeley. National myths were already running hot and heavy during the country's bicentennial, touting imperial grandeur wrapped in noble innocence. Dan, however, was talking about America in terms of Babylon, reading John's Revelation and the newspaper synoptically.

I was a new convert to the faith, intrigued by the Bible but aghast at the church and searching for some version of the tradition with backbone and balls. I left that evening knowing I'd heard a gospel to be reckoned with. I was never the same. Dan became a mentor, true north on my discipleship compass.

To put it plainly: Many of us would not be members of the North American faith-based justice and peace movement were it not for Dan's showing and telling of the gospel. For five decades he has opened political spaces through public witness, ignited theological imagination with his pen, and given us language of sanity and grace in a time when lies are sovereign. These kaleidoscopic gifts have helped us find enough courage to embrace something of the Way.

Exodus is the latest in Dan's venerable series of biblical reflections in which he blows the dust off sacred scrolls long buried in the cellars of a compromised church, blinks bemusedly at our pretenses of discipleship, and refuses to concede an inch to imperial shock and awe. It is vintage stuff from a prophetic reader of prophetic texts.

~

The last thing the Risen Jesus said to his disciples, before he was swooped like Elijah up into the heavens, was that the life and death of the church would depend upon its biblical literacy. Luke's Emmaus Road story reports that "beginning with Moses and all the prophets, Jesus interpreted the scriptures to the disciples" (Luke 24:27). The verb here is *diermēneuen*, an intensification of the word from which we derive "hermeneutics" (the art of interpretation). In every other appearance of this verb in the New Testament it means "to translate from one language to another" (Acts 9:36), especially the interpretation of ecstatic tongues (1 Cor 12:30; 14:5, 13, 27). The Risen Jesus is, in other words, portrayed here as a patient *translator* of counterintuitive biblical wisdom into a parlance that his demoralized disciples can fathom.

This inaugural Bible study in the history of the church makes it clear that the prophetic tradition should be the lens through which we make sense of our national history. Israel's prophets were forever engaging the way things were with the vision of what should be: questioning authority, picketing palaces, refusing to settle, interrupting business as usual, speaking truth to power, giving voice to the voiceless, stirring up the troops.

The prophets were accused of treason in times of warmaking for being an inconvenient conscience, and were inevitably jailed, exiled, or killed. Only after they were disposed of did they become nostalgic celebrities, honored with national holidays and street names. As in our own context with Martin, César, Dorothy, even Dan's own brother Phil once canonized, thereafter ignored. Nevertheless, insists Jesus, it is these very prophets who teach us how the sacred story should be read. Their witness, though first maligned and then mystified by those in power, represents the "hermeneutic key" to the *whole tradition*.

Luke reiterates this point later in Jesus' upper room appearance to the cowering disciples. "Then he *opened* their minds, that they might *understand* the scriptures" (Luke 24:45). The two verbs here tell an interesting story. *Dianoigō* elsewhere in the New Testament refers to the opening of deaf ears (Mark 7:34f), of a closed womb (Luke 2:23), of blind eyes (Luke 24:31), or of a hardened heart (Acts 16:14). The verb "to understand," meanwhile (*suniemi*), means to bring together all the data—to "connect the dots," so to speak. In the New Testament it is usually employed to describe those many situations in which disciples are *unable* to make such connections (e.g., Luke 2:50; 18:34; Acts 7:25). Both verbs are specifically connected in the gospels with the story of the call of Isaiah (Isa 6:8–10), in order to remind us that the reason we fail to understand the prophetic Word is ultimately because we are unable or unwilling to change our way of life.

The prophets exhort us to defend the poor; but we lionize the rich. ' They assure us that chariots and missiles cannot save us; yet we seek refuge under their cold shadow. They urge us to forgo idolatry; but we compulsively fetishize the work of our hands. Above all, the prophetic Word warns us that the way to liberation in a world locked down by the spiral of violence, the way to redemption in a world of enslaving addictions, the way to genuine transformation in a world of deadened conscience and numbing conformity, is the way of nonviolent, sacrificial, creative love. But neither polite religion nor society is remotely interested in this—which is why Jesus had to "translate" and "midwife" the prophetic insights for his companions in their historical moment.

Dan has done the same for us in ours. As this reading of Exodus attests, he has a keen eye for both text and context, and exegetes both with his life. Thus does he help us shed our denial, connect the dots, and move from our pews to the streets.

~

The unique poetry of both Dan's words and deeds has made an extraordinary impact. It has animated discipleship communities of resistance and renewal to an extent none of us can tally or fully fathom. In particular, he and his co-conspirators singularly helped rehabilitate the prophetic tradition of embodied symbolism in public space. For this Dan holds a special place in the history of social change movements.

Actions at Catonsville (1968) and again at King of Prussia (1980) rattled the dry bones of American opposition culture to life again. These powerful and provocative experiments in making the Word flesh represented a watershed in the tradition of nonviolent direct action. Homemade napalm and carpenter's hammers became ciphers that unmasked the Powers:

"Forgive us for burning paper instead of children."

"To beat swords into plowshares the hammer must fall."

Such symbolic action and explanation remind us that mere rational discourse does not suffice to challenge the murderous reign of technocracy. Such witness, from the Pentagon to arms factories, helped knit bones of conscience back together in the valley of death.

Bill Kellermann (a Methodist disciple of our Jesuit) rightly called such actions "public liturgy," and it stands to reason that they would have been born out of a priestly imagination. Dan's redeployment of the old sacred stuff of blood or ashes renewed our sacramental tradition and changed forever the way we view our Christian vocation of evangelism before the Powers (Eph 3:10).

Meanwhile, Dan's literary corpus has undergirded his prophetic embodiments, maintaining a mystical vision at the heart of strategic public gestures. The perennial temptation for activists is to force the connection between organizing and efficacy; to evaluate our work according to empirical results; to link hope (or despair) to this or that drift in the political current. Dan, on the other hand, is always insisting—it threads throughout this reading of Exodus—that there is no simple relationship between our initiative and divine redemption. With Gandhi we must remember that we sow seeds only, and leave the fruits to God. Between our deeds and our dreams is an opaque veil of unknowing, the consciousness of which keeps us from becoming that which we oppose. This is why we should always endeavor, as one of Dan's riddles put it, to say "yes and no to the whole damn thing."

Because Dan understands the difference between the "dead letter" of managerial logic and the life-giving Spirit of political imagination (2 Cor 3:6), his writing and acting tend toward the parabolic. This is one of his most animating gifts to us, impoverished as we are by capitalism's relentless advertising fantasies, commodity fetishism, and religious spiritualizing. If the social function of parables is to "deconstruct" and "reconstruct" consciousness, then Dan is a master craftsman.

Theologians rightly insist that all language about God is necessarily metaphorical, an assertion that deeply offends modernists, rationalists, and imperial engineers. But the truth is, *only* metaphors—carefully chosen and preferably biblically grounded—are strong enough to bear the horrors of the militaristic State, elastic enough to encompass the divine dream of liberation, and big enough to surround our deepest hopes and fears. Nothing less can inspire and sustain action that would be simultaneously revolutionary, nonviolent, and humane. Critical analysis, philosophical idealism, or ideological fervor alone cannot hold together the personal and the political, the past and the present, the prophetic and pastoral.

Dan's mediation of undomesticated mystery is thus deeply priestly, offering a refuge for imagination that cannot be locked down by the dehumanizing structural adjustments, technological messianism, or scientific demythologizing wrought by the totalitarian ideology of Progress. Dan continues to insist that Pharaoh let the people go. But he long ago up and left for the wilderness.

~

The last time I saw Dan was in 2003 at a Catholic Worker retreat in California (though I pray there might be another meeting yet, I am mindful of his eighty-six years). He was walking us through a poignant reading of Jeremiah 36. It struck me then that Dan himself is a kind of American Baruch. Like Jeremiah's amanuensis, he listens carefully to the prophetic Word; inscribes it lovingly; declares it publicly; and accompanies it underground when it is pronounced heretical to the logic of national security (Jer 36:15–19). And if and when the rulers of State or church contemptuously whittle the scrolls of truthtelling into the courtroom firepit, Dan obeys the mandate to write it all down again, over and over for as long as the denial prevails (Jer 36:20–28). In this way he has faithfully embodied the vocation of "reading of America biblically" inherited from William Stringfellow, Abraham Hesche, and Thomas Merton, with the accompaniment of Irish mystics and Jesuit martyrs.

I believe there is a sort of poetic justice that, at this stage of his life, Dan would turn his attention to Exodus. This wise, old wild tale speaks exactly to our historical moment (as it did equally for early Christians and desert monks and radical reformers and Abolitionists), particularly to resurgent perceptions of American omnipotence. Exodus is "biased beyond doubt," Dan points out; "it dwells compassionately on those left out of the imperial records" (see page 3 below). It is, as such, good news for the poor, and a warning to the Project for a New American Century and their ilk.

To be sure, Dan refuses to gloss over the difficult parts of Exodus, from the curious vignette in which Yahweh tries to kill Moses (31) to the texts of terror that seem to represent "an invitation to genocide" (164).

Indeed, Dan's reading ends on a note of ambiguity: "A shadow stands and will not dissolve" (161ff). Yet "our story must include its own version of the sins of Exodus" (159). For each character in this ancient epic is archetypal; the epic's setting amidst empire and its discontents is distressingly contemporary; and its plot of surprise and deliverance is still the stuff of hope.

What better companion, then, with whom to wrestle again with the ecstatic and traumatic tale of Exodus than this poet, practitioner, and priest? Dan is rightly revered among us. He is an oak of an elder: skin as thick as bark, leaves that can prick, a reach that defies gravity, providing cover for whoever would sit with him. He has been a kind of *axis mundi* in our lives, offering communion with both heaven and earth. And we need trustworthy elders as much as we do the saints, to pass on understanding like an heirloom. Again I say: We would not be here but for Dan's faithful work and witness over half a century. I honor him without apology. And I commend to you his reading of our oldest sacred narrative of liberation, which still beckons us to freedom.

Ched Myers
Sept 11, 2007

Exodus 1–3

My attempt at transcending scholarship is simply a literary critic's final reliance upon her or his own sense of a text, or what I have called the necessity of misreading. No critic, whatever her or his moldiness or skepticism, can evade a Nietzschean will to power over a text, because interpretation is at last nothing else.[1]

—*Harold Bloom, American literary critic*

A passion; to make the text mine.
Better, by assumption, maybe by impertinence, to make it—ours.

—*D. B.*

Oral culture is "verbomotor." Exclusively oral peoples are utterly unaware of anything like a neutral world. Primeval chaos is never far distant, nor is death. Everything they are familiar with is committed, noisy, and passionate for good or ill. . . .

And [that is] why sounds in general and words in particular are felt as powerful and dynamic actions to which a practical, canny response of action is required in return . . . .

Given the essential dynamism of a sound world as it issues reports of the spirit world—in thunder, flood, wind and voice—one can understand why the word of God . . . is a word of power. The Hebrew sense is paradigmatic. "My word, is it not like fire, a hammer that shatters the rocks?" (Jer 23:29).[2]

—*David Toolan, SJ*

~

So we begin; or more to the point of Exodus, so we continue. Or (closer to the "orality" of the people and Moses, and before the written word became a final arbiter of what events will live on, and what recede)—so we too go forth.

~

The contradiction will be damocleian sharp, and humiliating to boot. The thunders broke, and Yahweh spoke. One writes of this, but at second or third—or thousandth—remove. It is by no means guaranteed to the author that the thunders broke—on him; or that Yahweh spoke—to him.

The commentator remains safely sequestered in words, words, like a cocoon dreaming of birth—or perhaps like an academic in the famous groves, dreaming of whatever such eminences dream of. Tenure? A crown of laurel?

The text in sum, invites a woeful deconstruction of bombarding realities. So, one thinks ruefully, is the soul deconstructed in the act of writing—a task looked on (and so rightly) as the original artful dodge.

~

At least let the investigator keep a measure of good sense, walk humbly, conscious of ironies, hearing to his own discomfiture (and benefit), the sound of divine laughter.

Intemperate mirth? It well may be. And this, knowing that the rollicking One, as far as is known, never wrote a word—indeed is known famously and obscurely (but tellingly to our purpose), as Pure Act.

"I don't know, I'm not sure" . . . the would-be equivalent of a confession. Confess it then; woe to the scrivener, perpetually outside the action.

~

EXODUS 1

At the bravura of our narrator we are in awe, and rightly. His scope and bias are intact, even in conveying the mental confabulations and schemes of omnipotent pharaoh.

~

Much has been made of the identity of this notorious Egyptian regent. Was he Seti I or Meneptha or Rameses II? According to Exodus 12:40, the exile in Egypt lasted for 430 years. So we are face to face with a dynasty, or even with several of these.

But the above details are ignored by our author. The pharaoh is presented as a stereotype, a stone face on a frieze, an automaton going about his wicked, fussy, ultimately bootless works and pomps.

Before us is a particular, perhaps unique form of historical writing. Biased beyond doubt, it dwells compassionately on those left out of the imperial records, those of little or no account. In social upheaval and discomfiture of the mighty, "Those" become "These."

~

What then of the ruler, the pharaoh? Let him be irretrievably put down. Let him be not so much as named or pointed out from (one might think) a succession of his likes—before, during, since.

How the mighty are deflated before our eyes—and again and again how the lowly, the victims, are exalted! The names of two midwives, on whom depends all the future, are carefully recorded; shortly they will confound Pharaoh Anonymous I and his edicts.

~

To our author, the imperial one is an "emperor of ice cream." A veritable sun god in the eyes of his votaries melts before our eyes, is reduced, all but dismissed, a type, a cliché.

And in contrast, the invincible dignity, the saving arrogance of the underdog. We are being told, and this from the start of enforced bondage, that the mighty are in fact moral clones, their methods predictably awful. They make war. They are boundless in greed and appetite. They waste human lives in forced labor and the lash. Slaves, and a slave culture, is their perverse intent.

~

Patience. Wait and see. There are always "buts," a buttressing counter weight pressing against awful events and their agents. The weight will fall and bring the mighty down.

~

"He who acquires a slave, acquires a master."

—*Talmud*

~

Problems arise, even for pharaohs—perhaps especially for such. Let them create a system judged impermeable against chance and fate. On the drawing board of counselors, planners, diplomats, generals, millionaires, the system has no seams, no cracks. It is huckstered and put in place.

But . . . but—a question: how maintain that status quo, plausible, mighty as it stands?

~

Eccolo,[3] all in secret—but perceived by wise slaves (indeed by them brought to pass!)—there comes a night of resolve, a sea change under the moon. Roles are slowly, ever so subtly reversed. There dawns on the slaves, the truth of their lives; we are in bondage.

Then a second insight, equally valuable, equally dangerous; this woeful condition of ours need not be.

And what of those invincibles, the masters, overseers, owners? Time passes, in the palace fear grows, and a dark uncertainty. Fear of the victims. A muttering is heard, by a few, then by many. The slaves forge a code language.

~

Action, reaction. To keep the multitudes in check, law and order must stiffen. Public "examples" must be created, spectacles of punishment, the taws descending, prisons, starvations, executions. Slaves, See and learn!

Nothing avails.

Then, on to a draconian "solution." They breed like magpies, these slaves. Law must strike at the source, the wellspring of life. Kill the newly born.

~

In view of the above royal rake's progress, from lesser crime to greater, why, asks our scribe, why identify by name this or that oppressor? Each is a stranger to wisdom or compassion. Each is unfit for rule.

Who then shall be judged worthy of emulation and praise? The word of God looks elsewhere than the throne. To a coven of lowly Hebrew women. And we are instructed.

~

This affair of naming, misnaming, naming aright, withholding a name. A small matter on the face of it; but to the Bible, clearly of first import. The power is primordial; naming reality is the first task assigned the first human:

> When the Lord God had formed out of the ground all the beasts
> of the fields and the birds of the air, be brought them to the man
> to see what he would name them.
>> For that which the man would call each of them would be its
> name.
>> The man named all the cattle, all the birds of the air and all the
> beasts of the field . . .
>
> —Gen 2:19

~

The word of God names things aright. More: according to that word, those who are literate in the word, know that a like task is handed over. To ourselves.

Let us (the scribes) be careful to name reality aright, honoring the instruction of Genesis.

The exiled midwives are named. Thus their lives, the risks they enter on, the compassion of their hands—these are underscored. Note is taken, and honor paid a noble resistance.

Pause then, pay tribute, as does the text. Salute their courage; courage too is commended to us. May they strengthen our resolve, as we too face the 'law of the land', that famous artificer of—misnaming.

~

Scrutinize, ponder, then name aright.

Let us call on the holy women for intercession. Life in America being a parlous middle passage, between Scylla and Charybdis; "Lying" to the left of us, "Masking" to the right.

~

Another point, and a capital one. Since the dawn of Genesis, and passim in Exodus, our astonishing chronicler hesitates not at all to convey the mind of God. Thus sayeth Yahweh!—a genius puts words in the mouth of the holy One—decree, denunciation, blame, accusation, fury. And now and again, praise of this or that favorite.

And how rarely is heard a word of love . . .

Under a magisterial hand, Yahweh emerges in the text, wild of eye, brutal of arm, vastly ranging as to influence and act. And beyond predicting. A god befitting a tribe of untamed nomads. A nomad god.

The eye of the scribe rests on the Eye, so to speak. And a ready wit is close to hand. Quite a genius, and how daring!

~

As to the pharaoh, uneasy lies the head. This eminence must be ever vigilant, lest his drudges slip the tether. In the present instance, the danger is manifest—an explosion of births among the slaves.

On the face of it, one would think a burgeoning populace would be of advantage to the owners. More producers, consumers, workers, weapons bearers, hoplites!

True, but another possibility lurks. Males, born in ever larger numbers, become troublesome, erupt; and this especially if a war break out—an ever present possibility in the empire.

~

Thus goes the "worst case" scenario, an imperial nightmare, an enemy at the gates. And within, insurrection. And then? Slaves exulting, slaves suddenly transformed to former slaves, havocking, avenging, breaking free.

In sum, exodus!

~

Rhetoric to the contrary, the boundaries of empire are thin and vulnerable. Troubled colonies abroad, resentment at home, a queasy economy, envy in the air.

Slaves? Of course, these are the fundament and capstone of empire. The pharaonic projects are grandiose, and require massive labor. But strict control above all, in works and numbers.

~

Interesting is the implied comment "from below," on the machinations of the Olympians. The narrator is a friend of the slaves; indeed he descends from them.

And this friend of the enslaved knows the mind of the slave master as well.

~

It could hardly be sensible to relay to drudges the troubled ruminations of the pharaoh and the palace claque. Even less sensible to announce an imminent, awful decree.

No, keep them in ignorance. Is harsh duress about to descend, and if so, what form will it take? Uncertainty regarding personal and social fate is a prime ingredient of bondage.

So the palace to-fro and its conclusions are communicated solely to a few. A decree is formulated, it reaches only those in charge.

And what of those immediately affected, the slaves? Do they sense an atmosphere grown charged, ominous? All to the good.

~

Thus early on, in our story the attitude of great prophets vis-à-vis tyrants, is at work. An image of the pharaoh emerges. It diminishes before our eyes. Hardly omnipotent, as claimed. Quite the opposite: a chronic worrier and schemer, small-minded, heartless.

Preposterous even. Under the astringent eye of the chronicler, his power is unmasked, then derided.

How wonderfully unsubdued he is, our historian, as though in a quiet voice admonishing his people; be unsubdued!

From his hand emerges a properly religious history, which is to say, a history favoring, cherishing the victims. Implying—and at times strongly stating—that there exists another Power, in face of which the machinations of the pharaohs are both futile and foolish.

~

> It is only when one wishes the impossible that one remembers
> God. To obtain that which is possible, one turns to those like
> himself.[4]
>
> —*Lev Shestov, Russian philosopher*

~

According to the author of Exodus, these are the dynamics of imperial power. First (as suggested before), the system absolutely requires slaves. The enslavement must be absolute. Its ingredients: harsh, degrading labor, enforced ignorance and passivity. And finally, (male) births must be limited.

(The Herods, it would seem, have a long ancestry. On occasion, their prospering too demands the killing of the newborn).

~

"Who can withstand the beast?" (Rev 13:4). The political and military systems imply omnipotence and immortality. Shows of force abound, public humiliation, trials and executions. Unmistakable examples!

Further, as goes without saying—the "system" lies beyond critique by its victims—let alone beyond challenge. Tight lips make for safe, unutterably wretched lives.

Politically correct images are also crucial, images of invincible power. Historians, poets, architects, visual artists are enlisted, in service of The Invincible Image—judicious, recondite creations, colossal totems, temples and shrines, victory arches, steles and their inscriptions. Thus artists and artisans, chroniclers and poets, magians of hand and eye produce works and pomps of deification.

~

With regard to slaves and forced laborers, the images serve another end: they forge the chains anew. They deepen, even spiritualize, the enslavement. Are multitudes stripped of dignity and status? Yes. Will their progeny exist in a like predicament, forever and ever? Yes. Such is simply the will of whatever god.

The idolatrous images tower over; the slaves grow numb and hopeless. Now slavery becomes a sublimely simple and seamless matter: the will of the gods. Injustice has reached from heaven to earth. Validated.

Is the imperial system unjust? Metaphysically so. For its gods are unjust.

~

The images, we note, are static and yet superhuman. They infer a definition of time. For the enslaved, time is a stalemate. And for those in command, the images imply conquest over time. The pharaoh is immortal, son of the sun god. His symbols? The great pyramid, brobdingnagian, grand and mysterious in its perfection. And the sphinx, stonewalling, saying nothing. Knowing as she does, everything.

~

This word in sum for the slaves; "You are who you are—and you shall be who you are." This is the iron law announced by the images.

Our tale opens; half a millennium of enslavement has passed. Is this not proof of the perdurance of the slave superstate? The system surpasses time and aborts change.

~

The word of God must go counter. Thus one commentator writes (undoubtedly in reference to the Hebrew Bible):

> The Bible is not a work of art in the same sense as a poem. It is not meant primarily to make an intellectual demand in memorable language—or like Greek myth to tell an absorbing story, or like Greek tragedy to purge us by pity and terror. It aims to move us to justice and mercy. It is *active* art, to which people trust their conduct; moral art, which (rightly or wrongly), designates some form of violence as necessary for the conduct of ethical social life.[5]

—*Catherine Madsen, American writer and editor*

~

Slaves must face squarely the hard truth of their condition. Drumming it in; this is the first subversive act of the "peoples' history," the story of Exodus. "No getting used to injustice, no coming to terms with it." Thus the counter to the law of images.

The second act is more daring, more dangerous. It announces in plain terms that the imperial images are in reality, a clutch of illusions.

Subversion, deflation. The truth goes counter; rumors start. The pharaohs are mortal like ourselves. So is the regime mortal. It will flourish for a while and flaunts its greatness. But it will decline and fall. If not in our lifetime, then after.

Believe it. Help it happen! The system is subject to a law that governs all mortal enterprises—a law of transience and death.

~

Thus the pharaonic images are summoned to judgment, condemned as deceitful and destructive. Slaves, note the imperative. The images must be exorcised, banished from the slave community.

And a second imperative. The images must be replaced. Summon other images, stories, lives, possibilities, anodynes, strengths. These two above all; first, the image of a God other than the gods of the overlord. Then, an image of the truly human, those who are neither slaves nor slavemasters. Those who walk free.

A liberating God, and liberated humans. That is it! An image of the God of the ancestors, who intervened on behalf of Abraham, Isaac, Jacob. Of a God who, though people be guilty of moral setback and sin, never abandoned his own, took their part, reproved, chastened, stood with, walked beside.

The counter-image, drawn from a common wellspring of story recounted and worship enacted—these lighten the burden of life at the bottom.

Someone lifts the yoke! The purport of the redeeming images is irresistible, a liberating God and a command; Freedom Now!

And—a Moses.

～

Thus, despite a seeming dead end of exile and bondage, despite the mindless might of the overlords, the overbearing law of the land—powerless as you are, a clutch of slaves seemingly void of recourse—nonetheless believe. Your salvation nears.

Someone. Whisper the name. Moses.

～

EXODUS 2

At hand, a savior? It is all but ludicrous, a mirage in the night. Lately a decree has been issued, commanding the death of male infants. Death, upon this sole offense: having been born.

But the decree, as things turn, has gone too far. The comatose, the near hopeless, awaken to a rage that had been all but quenched. Resist, let us resist!

～

Women ponder: Shall we undo the murderous decree, shall we commit the "crime" of safe birth and rescuing? Such works will be hard and perilous.

Nonetheless a few midwives conspire. Two among them are singled out, Shiphrah and Pua.

Their profession is noble, and honored as such: to assist new life into the world. What part then shall they, the abettors of life, have in killing?

Purpose holds firm. They disobey. New life! They answer secret summonses, go on with their work.

The pharaoh hears of it, hails them in for an accounting: Why have they not followed orders? Because they "fear God," is the author's gloss on their holy disobedience.

Their response is a simple equivocation; delicious.

> The
> Hebrew women
> are not
>> like
> the Egyptian women.
>> These
> are robust
> and
> give birth
> before
> the
> midwife arrives. (Exod 1:19)

The pharaoh is omnipotent, omniscient, or so it is said. But lo! he is suddenly, strangely helpless. His hands drop. He neither prosecutes nor imprisons nor kills the malfeasants. He dare not; they are held in high esteem among the slaves. How shall he counter their hedging?

He and his decree are stalemated. He shifts tactics, issues a general order. It sounds much like a confession of defeat.

Now hear this, a command "to all his people"; they are obliged, on discovery, to cast newborn Hebrew males in the Nile.

~

Birth and death, contention—then a kind of rebirth; valiant midwives, infants snatched from death. Through holy disobedience the law of the land is thwarted. The good news passes like a wildfire!

The image of the midwives bespeaks a modest, irrefutable strength. Their acts are a summons, a contamination: Arise!

Their example beckons others, into uncharted danger, chance-taking. And above all, lifting of the spirit!

~

The great moment nears: the birth of a people, prefigured, imminent, in the protected birth of infants.

In the protected birth of a national hero and savior.

So momentous an event comes only through pain and reversal. The hero must be literally snatched from death.

~

The ingenuity and courage of women! Some few, as we have noted, are named; the midwives, together with Miriam, sister of the infant. (Of her, along with brother Aaron, much will be heard later). And mother Jocabed, who launched the newborn in his craft among the reeds.

And surely another subversive detail—the daughter of the pharaoh is drawn into the web of mercy. Subversive mercy has reached far and high, into the palace itself.

~

The genealogy of the future prophet is short, instructively so. No remote ancestry is traced, the parents only are named. The father of Moses: Amram. The mother: Jochebed (Exod 6:20).

The omissions are heavy with implication. Let this story be concentrated, sharp, close. A few names only. Read them, commit them to memory; these few will shape an astonishing future.

A further irony, and what a credential! The name of the child is conferred by the pharaoh's own daughter. He is called Moses, perhaps, it is suggested, as an Egyptian cover.

And we marvel. In the land of oppression, all unwitting, a Hebraism is adroitly conferred; which is to say, a name that infers a vocation. Not "the one drawn from the water," as the putative mother would have it—but "the one drawing water." An ironic reference, one ventures, to the tasks of a slave people, "hewers of wood, drawers of water."

~

Legends parallel to the saving of infant Moses were current in other cultures and times. Romulus and Remus, Cyrus, and most ancient of all, Sargon, were drawn out of mortal danger in infancy.

So is Jesus to be drawn, and barely.

~

Turn and turnabout. Infant Moses is snatched from the Nile, his mother is hired as nurse; everything dovetails wonderfully. And when the child is weaned, Jocabed gives him back to the pharaoh's daughter, who proceeds to raise him as her own son.

The arrangement is satisfactory, one thinks, for all concerned. The king's daughter, as far as can be known, is childless; now she has a son, to all appearances a native child graced with an Egyptian name.

And Jocabed can also rejoice. What safer haven for an endangered son than the arms of the king's daughter?

~

The story races along. Moses reaches adulthood, draws closer to his daunting vocation: savior of his people. Passed over in silence are the years of childhood. In view of what is to come, these do not signify.

Yet we long to know more. What of the education of young Moses? Who were his mentors? What studies did he undertake? Did an Egyptian education alienate him from his own?

And what was the impact of these years on the events he would initiate under God, this progenitor, lawgiver, mystic, instructor of his people? What resources gathered in the soul of a survivor, what courage to initiate and command, what singleness of mind, what self understanding—such qualities as would fit him to counter the pharaoh?

And what virtues would enable him to endure the desert years to come, the squabbling people, the encounters, face to face, with The One Who Is?

Of all this, our story tells nothing. The child, the youth might be a typically favored Egyptian scion, taking emoluments and luxuries for granted, blindsided by fortune.

~

The orality of a people offers a clue. The text is all movement, abruptness. "Speed to the point, the climax; get on with it," is the motto of Exodus. The text is racing, energetic, even antic.

Prepare to be astonished, set off kilter. Read as you run. Do not be troubled if this or that matter (of intense interest to yourself!) is ignored. Focus on a storyteller without peer. Enter his mind and intent, read between the lines. And give him large credit. He knows something you do not; he invites you to ponder.

~

Thus the story forms from within. Whatever is included is worthy of probing and pondering; move with its implications, hints, analogies. Give the author time and space. Following where so sure a guide leads, you will come to know (to a degree!) who this Moses is, what motive impels him.

~

The start of the great tale is an infant's outcry amid the reeds of the Nile, a voice that, one day, will shake the world.

A helpless infant, not abandoned, is greatly loved, protected by high and low. To become—only give him time—the liberator.

Helpless? Infant? A greater than the pharaoh, a greater than a dynasty of pharaohs, is here.

~

In the Acts of the Apostles, Stephen, the Deacon, reviewing sacred history in presence of the Sanhedrin, says only that Moses "was instructed in all the wisdom of the Egyptians" (Acts 7:22).

Some would even have it that our emerging hero is a native Egyptian. The snatching from the Nile is seen as a common type of "hero story." A more or less fictive savior, larger than life, is saved, surrounded by loving care, and flourishes.

What ironies are captured in a few narrative phrases! In the shadow of the destroyer, a savior approaches his hour. His will be a salvation story, a momentous beginning, comparable in its way to the first week of creation.

~

And the grand choreography of the exodus begins with—a murder. The fires of liberation are kindled by an evil deed. The savior is also of the race of Cain, no mistaking it.

The episode is laconically set down, tellingly so. The hero must undertake a kind of personal exodus, crucial, a first step, a larger second, a third still more momentous—and so on.

This for simple start: Moses

"went to visit his kinsmen."

Went from where? From a palace, one thinks; or at least from a place of secure comfort, if not luxury.

~

And what meets his eye, as he issues, perhaps for the first time, in public? Misery, forced labor, the inhuman decrees of the pharaoh in bitter play. A lash, his people bowed to the earth in humiliation.

~

Young Moses has been favored, privileged and apart, he has suffered nothing of duress and wounding. An innocent abroad. Then, as our author would have us know, a brutal sight met his eyes.

Education? One lesson, and he knew. His world exploded. Now he could say, and rue and rejoice at the knowledge, "These are my people."

And a judgment fell like a hammer blow: "Those are not my people." Inescapable; if a larger world is to be embraced, a former life must be rejected.

~

Time too is changed. The imperial system, that immutable form of the future, is shaken.

Assurance has been seemingly invincible. Moses child, Moses youth. He is, always will be, well fed and housed, esteemed. The palace was a nursery, not a school. Or if a school, its curriculum aimed at the stalemating of moral maturity.

Done with all that, and no returning. Choose. You have been chosen.

~

Verse 11 and following

One day, we are told, the youth walked out. And shortly, reality struck. He witnessed the corvée, the abuse. Overmastered with fury, he stepped over a boundary:

> He saw
> an Egyptian
> striking a Hebrew,
>
> one
> of his own kin.
>
> And
> he raised
> a weapon,
>
> and
> killed. (Exod 2:11–12)

He killed the decree as well, as it fell on "his brothers." The decree fell on himself: he, the exempted, a Hebrew graced (or cursed) with an Egyptian name. Prospering, silent, a corvée of silence. Silence—the "forced labor" imposed on him.

Isolated, at distance from "my brothers." Then he killed. He killed the decree as well, and its sway over his life. He killed, and

"buried (the corpse) in the sand" (Exod 2:12).

~

And what of the mother and father, how do they fare, what shame is theirs, as Moses leaves for parts unknown, a fugitive? What of the pharaoh's daughter, upon whom must fall the onus of his crime and the anger of her father?

Nothing of these grievous matters, not a word. The story is single-minded. The hero is the point, very nearly the only point. Parents, putative mother, no matter how tight the bonds, these are minor players in the Saga of the Hero.

~

Moses recoils from the scene of death. And the story follows close. He becomes for a time a wanderer, a killer known to the authorities, a Cain with a price on his head.

Thus the inauspicious beginning, make of it what we will:

> He saw
> an Egyptian
> striking a Hebrew,
>
> one
> of his own
> kinsmen. (Exod 2:11)

Still, granted the provocation—what to make of the murderous start? What good can come of this?

~

After Moses, the grand saga of patriarchs continues. Other personages appear. And violence, betrayal, envy, greed, murder—these are the dark motif, the anti-*shekinah* over all.

THE LAND OF THE FRANKS

> It was at the worst crossroads of my journey;
> on one path, venomous flames licking up from the abyss;
> on the other, the shunned regions
> where nausea swelled within me
> at everything people praised and practiced.
> I derided their gods, and they mine . . .
>
> Then a fabulous call summoned me . . . of the unrecognized and hounded-out...

How often of late, when I had already gained ground
struggling in my gloomy homeland
and not yet certain of victory
a whisper has lent me new strength . . .[6]

    —*Stefan George, German poet*

≈

Exiled, young Moses must bide awhile. An exile in Egypt, now he is a forced exile in Midian, a land of strangers not far from fabled Mount Sinai.

Finally a light breaks; the somber prelude yields to a pastoral dawn. The outcast discovers a lover and spouse, Sepphora. She bears him a son, Gersam.

≈

A wife and son, both Midians, outsiders—how will these be received among his own?

But who are his own? Are we not subtly being told—salvation will come through a radical outsider?

≈

Every hero must depart from home. The furious breakthrough of young Moses, together with the distance he must travel—far from privilege—this renunciation is a harsh measure indeed.

Cannily, the storyteller places the departure against another measure—his return, the worth of an appointed task, gradually revealed.

≈

Reaching so ideally high, adhering so adamantly to noble principles and what he called "purity of means," Gandhi failed to achieve all he hoped for India. But the passion of his life was the legacy he left to his country and to the world, inspiring millions with the grandeur of his dream and some few disciples with an ardent love of suffering on their own painfully narrow road to martyrdom. In Gandhi's passion lies the key to his inner temple of pain . . .

And through the multifaceted prism of his passion, Gandhi's tragic weakness is revealed as the other side of his singular strength, helping to account for his final failure to win that for which he worked hardest and suffered most.[7]

—*Stanley Wolpert, American historian*

∾

A law is promulgated; it bears a double edge. It favors (and opposes) a spirit whom adversity will harden to Damascene.

And the law touches all. Ourselves.

We, and our near ruin, must be measured against young Moses. Our ruin? The Fall; our near incapacity that is, to overcome slavery, to shake off bondage. To walk away from the realm of Necessity, whose regent is a pharaoh, keeper of slaves. The one who, if his realm is to prosper, must ensure that the slaves be kept slaves.

He has death in mind. For sake of his system, he would have us destroyed—if not in infancy, later. But destroyed. Dignity, compassion, care for one another, obliterated. A sense of God, of providence, of civility and mutuality, all defeated.

Do we dwellers in Egypt seek an "improved" a "better" system, a "reformed," a system of mitigated enslavement, lesser wars?

If the search is legitimate, if it makes sense, if the reform of Egypt can be thought to succeed—then the exodus is proven redundant.

But the search for an "improved empire" is witless, and bound to fail. That "better system" cannot be summoned. There are no stories in our Bible to tell of such an event, to justify the effort. A mirage. Take note, American liberals, American Catholics, theologians, and "just war" phantasists.

∾

In an ancient empire, a prophet receives his commission from on high. In the order of "things to be done," a fearsome emphasis, doubled, rests on the negative.

One named Jeremiah is commanded

to pluck up

and

to break down;

to destroy

and

to overthrow.

The NO! to things as they are is harsh, uncompromising, radical. Go to the roots. Not a word of reform, accommodation, gradualism or the like.

Then (but only then), after the fierce preliminary toppling, can a YES! be uttered in good faith.

Something new, structures in favor of "widows and orphans and strangers at the gate." A new will, from the ground up. The task is abruptly stated, compressed. Now the same Jeremiah is commanded

to build

and to plant. (Jer 1:10)

~

In our Christian testament do the dead tell stories—those whom Jesus must raise before they can utter a word?

To our ears, on the page of the gospel, they say never a word.

And with Moses, we are in predawn. Is it too early to raise the question, what stories the dead might tell?

Ask it anyway. You have a clue in the Exodus account. The equivalent dead, the race of slaves, against all odds will rise from death and tell their story.

Are we not then to embrace, and be embraced by, another tremendous Overcoming, those wounds that tell of death overcome—the wounds of resurrection?

~

In April 1990, Fr. Michael Lapsley was the target of a letter bomb from South Africa. A friend writes of the scene in hospital a few days after the blast:

The one to whom we had come to minister, was ministering to us. I saw Christ there. . . . Christ in pain. Christ with his hands blown off. Christ speaking to us through bleeding lips. Christ with one eye . . .

Yes, I saw Christ lying in that bed, and I felt Christ minister to me. It was one of the most extraordinary spiritual experiences of my life.

I saw not one sign of bitterness or hatred . . . I stood and could but watch and listen as this Christian drama took the form of human flesh—scarred, burnt, dismembered human flesh in the form of a friend, pastor, fellow priest and comrade.[8]

—*Michael Worsnip, May 7, 1990*

~

Before us stands young Moses, husband and father. Also, dare we forget (though to all appearances his god forgets), a murderer—probably with a price on his head.

Twice exiled—but no slave!—he is granted a vision of the God. And in that place and time a vocation is appointed.

Suddenly, and with no warning—but how could we be warned?— there is a God. Since the start of our story and the long enslavement in Egypt, we have heard little or nothing of this deity. What evidence we were given was sparse indeed; a series of disguises-in-action, deeds of a peculiar providence, hinted at through a veil of human interventions. A distant God, prescient, watching, biding time.

Was evidence secretly accreting, an unwonted act of compassion, an eye resting on the human scene with unwonted kindness? We ponder the merciful midwives, the kindness of pharaoh's daughter—a hint of some-one "other," gentle, compassionate, courageous, feminine in fact.

The hero was lifted from the waters. The saving gesture, a slight insult to the scheme of empire—then out and out, like an expanding ripple in the Nile. An ever so gentle whisper of waters. The innuendo seemed to be: cast aside differences of status, religion, gender. Let a human sense arise, let arms succor the vulnerable and victimized. Slave or free, Hebrew or Egyptian, let hearts respond to a child's wail. Save me!

And the saving act is presented as simply—human. Shiphrah, Puah, Amram, Jochebed and the daughter of Pharaoh, how astonishing they are! They create on the instant, for a lorn infant, a future.

They vindicate their humanity (and our own). In a contamination of mercy, they judge and convict the implacable "other," the pharaoh, his inhumane system, the bureaucrats and slave masters.

~

Of those midwives it was said only that they "feared God." This, the author avers—and surely with an eye toward us—is enough. Or ought to be.

The women "feared God." It is their sole credential. It is also thus far, the sole explicit "reference beyond" in our story.

To the intent of our author, it suffices.

What connection is drawn by these women, between saving infants and fearing God? Were they granted early on, an intuition to be uttered centuries later, by One who surely knew—to the effect that

> God
> is
> God
> of the living,
>   not
> of
> the
> dead? (Matt 22:32)

~

Verses 23–24

Now at length, lightning has struck. The divine intrudes, unmistakably. First, with a surge of pity for the enslaved,

> The Israelites groaned and cried out because of their slavery. As their cry for release went up to God, he heard their groaning and was mindful of his covenant with Abraham, Isaac and Jacob . . . (Exod 2:23)

~

EXODUS 3

Verse 1 and following

Now, on to the savior. Moses is to be dealt with (surely in more senses than one!).

Fire, and a Voice. No shocking epiphany here. Nor by any means a bodily appearance (that will wait—Jesus). Here the divine intrudes through the lowly things of this world. A flora becomes the nest of glory: a bush, inflamed, unconsumed.

And an altogether extraordinary exchange is recorded, remarkable for omissions as well as substance. This God, this transcendent remembering One, is also the forgetting One.

With regard to memories retained or set aside, the deity must be thought—selective. And, perhaps, above all, surprising.

~

Let us confess; we seek in the deity a consistency, a logic tighter than our own. And this, it seems, is a first error, perhaps a capital one. The god will reveal himself, witting or not, as a somewhat mixed blessing; malevolent at times, and avenging. In seeming whim he will choose and reject, embrace and cast aside.

And more, and worse; given time and occasion, he will create (or allow to be created in his name), a system of inside players and outsiders, victims.

~

As concerns young Moses and the corpse he has buried in the sand—the desert winds scour and level all. It is as though the deed were not. And the memory of the god is blank as an unmarked grave. Forgiveness, or default?

Did not the God's favorite strike down an Egyptian bully? Good riddance, is the implication. The hero, granted a fresh start, walks free.

The murder in Egypt is as if it were not. It is done with, no word of consequence. The Egyptian was no brother, he was an enemy, an oppressor of the helpless. Good riddance!

~

The god descends in a fiery epiphany. Moses must put aside his sandals. Unshod, he is cleansed in the flame, a new being.

On reflection, the sequence marks an extraordinary reversal; the logical ordering of crucial matters is reversed.

The first matter at hand is the task, the vocation. Then the self-revelation, the self-naming of the God. A voice, as yet unidentified, speaks. We have read of it before, recounted in the third person, that "hearing" from above (Exod 2:24–25).

The passage trails off, incomplete:

> He
> heard
> their groaning
>
> and was mindful
> of his covenant
>
> with Abraham,
> Isaac
> and Jacob.
>
> He saw
> the Israelites
>
> and
> knew . . .

Knew what? What the god knew, one concludes, the author in all probability knew. And like the god, preferred to keep the secret.

Now, direct, piercing, the voice is heard; authoritative, loud and clear;

> I
> have heard
>
> the plaints
> of my people . . .

It is

you

who

are appointed

to

lead

them

forth. (Exod 3:7, 10)

The charge is onerous, overwhelming. And for the first time, the ineffable "I" announces an identity.

Who might this "I" be? By what authority is Moses "sent"? Various traditions coalesce here, we are told. (One almost thought; various special interests collide!)

~

The pivot of what follows is a question; who speaks for the deity, who names the unnamable? Shall it be the priests? (We recall that the father-in-law Jethro is a priest, a nice detail dropped gently in the text.)

According to the priests, Abram was favored with knowledge of the Name, "El-Shaddai, God the Almighty." But the Yahwists hold fast to another name, hearkening back to a time before the deluge; simply, "the Lord" (Gen 4:26).

And now (to the Elohists and their witness Moses), in the unconsumed flame yet another name is spoken—"Yahweh." And an unimpeachable credential is adduced:

... the God
of Abraham,
of Isaac
and Jacob ...

This
is the Name

I shall bear
forever,

in which

all
generations

shall
name
Me. (Exod 3:15)

~

Access and distance both, the mystery. And controversy unending. Is the god here naming the god, is the god refusing to name the god?

A circle opens, a circle closes. Consent, one thinks, and refusal. In Exodus we undergo the first of a multitude of shocking surprises, issuing from the great Surpriser, the primal Shocker. This—you shall know Me, and in effect you shall know nothing of Me.

~

Those who claim a definitive naming here, a scene of close access (verging on control?)—let them beware. If they think to hold in possession the "medicine" of the god, to bend this one to their will, presumption will lead to great suffering. This God is no idol to be turned and turned about, disempowered, in service of custom or self-interest.

And likewise, let those beware who claim a refusal to name. They too will pay, in ignorance and confusion of mind. The evidence is plain, and hardly in their favor; the midrash, the underscored import of the Name, as though signed, sealed and delivered into the keeping of Moses—these stand against them:

This
is the Name

I

will

bear

forever. (Exod 3:15)

~

One matter stands beyond doubt—Moses is entrusted with a message, and a mandate as well. Will he also bear new news, an ineffable Name? The uncertainty will hoist generations on a petard; a dilemma, an "either-or," a "yes" and a "no."

We are to keep pronouncing, invoking the Name—and we know so little of the One who bears the Name. The God is in the world, and apart from the world. The God dwells in the fiery bush—and the God is neither fire nor bush. The Name rests on the tongue of Moses—and the One so named seals the mouth of the one who would speak it—reduces him to a stammer, a groan, tears.

~

It is all here in embryo—choice and consequence. And the timing is everything. Long after the revelation, the story is set down; the vast panorama of grandeur and shame and risk, the exodus, the story of the powerless who arise, arise—first like a spasm of Samson in chains, then in a mighty convergence of power assumed. Yes, we go from here!

It is written down centuries later, the luster and fame. Inevitably the tale has been colored, altered, tinged and tendentious with ideology. The memory is owned, the story told, by the rulers of imperial Jerusalem.

~

Shibboleths prevail. One after another, the awful kings of the chosen tribe mount the throne, seize on the God for their own, lay claim to an improbable ancestry of valor and virtue in Saul and David and Solomon.

Then the prophets appear and speak. Shakers of thrones, doubters, naysayers, they lay a corrective hand on the scroll. But for them, it would have only this to record; the exodus as seen centuries later by the kings of Judah and Jerusalem.

Which is to say, the era of beginnings is set down in an era of pretension, economic enslavement, war—of social, economic, yes religious systems, akin to those of imperial Egypt or Babylon.

~

Of crucial note, this—the author of Genesis and Exodus wrote toward the last years of Solomon, whose reign ended around 922 CE. And one wonders—does our literary genius stand in a kind of shamed collusion with the assimilationists, the kings of Israel?

After the aborted revolution of the Maccabees, three generations of clan wars achieved only this—creation of an apish imperium.

After that debacle, our text takes its final form.

~

If that were all, why open the scroll? Or why indeed compose it?

One ventures—by way of warning and sane prospect, both. In hope of other, better things to come. Other, far different consequences. Almost one thinks, a different species of humans walking our tormented world. The great prophets.

Who will salvage—something. Will prepare a way (as Christians believe)—for Someone.

~

Meantime, a salutary warning. In the centuries from Exodus through Judges and Kings, a violent leadership begets a double phenomenon: a war god in its own image, and a succession of ethical clones. The latter bear arms, kill wantonly, die in battle. Multitudes pay heavily for royal follies, in forced taxation, poverty, generational hatreds.

~

And today, at the turn of another millennium?

> You get what you pay for, and we are paying for war. When this war [in Kosovo] is over, the President, the Pentagon and the weapons makers and dealers will lobby congress using your tax dollars, to demand more of your tax dollars. They will call the NATO bombing a victory, will appeal to you to dig deep in your pockets to pay to replace the cruise missiles and the smart bombs,

and they will ask you to dig deeper still to buy the next generation of high tech weaponry. . . .

Our political and military leaders have persuaded congress to pay any price for military readiness, and we are all set for war. They refuse to pay a penny for peace readiness...

They think of peace in only two dimensions, pre-war and post-war.

We must engage in the long and difficult political work to open their eyes, to unclog their ears and to soften their hearts . . .[9]

—*Joe Volk, American activist*

~

An anti nuclear organization, Greenpeace, announced that it was sending a Dutch icebreaker, the Arctic Sunrise, to a "hazard zone" designated by the Air Force off the launching site at Vandenberg Air Force Base, Calif., to try to stop the test.

"Mr. President, you have the finger on the star wars button," Greenpeace wrote in a letter to Mr. Clinton. "We urge you to take it off and make the world a safer place."

. . . Fifty Nobel laureates have said that any movement to deploy a missile defense system would be "premature, wasteful and dangerous."[10]

—New York Times, *July 7, 2000*

~

We summon the era of the Hebrew prophets. A socialized, stalemated spirit prevails, people and rulers alike are stuck, "dwellers on earth."

And the prophets delight in stirring the pot and proffering a bitter brew of ironies. Imperial crime gives the lie to the claim, "we are the chosen." Isaiah and Jeremiah denounce the credential of the imperial god. It is fraudulent, a forgery, as the warrior-deity decrees that the stranger is the enemy, the enemy to be exterminated.

And whatever the short-term gains in "riches, honors and the credit of a great name," the shame abides, a stigma on the soul.

~

As for our story—Moses returns, in accord with the instruction from on high, to report to the elders in Egypt. The tone is laconic. It is as though he has been party to the most ordinary event in the world; a burning bush, a presence, Yahweh, and a message "to me (and to you)."

No beating about, so to speak, the bush. This is the word—through means yet to be revealed, chains are shortly to fall. And this, after some 450 years!

~

Verses 24 –26

Meantime, questions, questions. Do threats against other forms of sovereignty roil away, under the surface of the text? Is dread of insurrection, leading as it does to the decree against male births, yielding to a trope? Does this indecipherable Yahweh sense the rising of a rival star in the firmament, a planet named Moses?

Something of the above darkens the air. What follows is madly illogical, and shocking in the extreme. On the way from Madian to Egypt, the little entourage of Moses and family pauses for a night encampment. And in the small hours, without warning Yahweh (or the "angel of Yahweh"), attacks.

It is as though the fabric joining heaven and earth were rent by a murderous descent. A hand appears, tearing the arras of heaven; it bears a sword.

A scene out of Lorca, bathed in imagery of black and red, of night and blood.

Moses has killed; is the visitant an angel of retribution? Would the god destroy a killer? But hasn't the god, shortly before, chosen a killer, named him anew as savior of his people?

Let be. No brawny logic governs the darkness or the deed.

~

Wonderfully, the hand of the most high is stayed, and barely, by the hand of spouse Sepphora. She undertakes a mediating rite, the circumcision of her son. Will blood lust have blood? So be it; the blood of the infant will mitigate divine fury.

Exodus 1–3

It is the mother who performs the rite, as Moses apparently stands by. Is he petrified, stalemated?

Lucky Moses. His lady is forthright and intuitive. She improvises a ritual and placates the deity. Then she touches the sex of her spouse with the foreskin of the infant, saying:

> You are
>
> a spouse
> of blood
>
> to
> me. (Exod 4:25)

Her words are translated by some:

> Through
> blood,
>
> to me
>
> you
> are
> circumcised.

(In Arabic, the word for "spouse" is related to the word for "circumcision." Apparently from the beginning, the rite of circumcision was aimed at enabling marital activity.)

And Yahweh withdraws like an assassin into the night.

~

A preemptive strike from the heavens? The message perhaps: "Come not too near!" Or, "Be like me, but be not too much like me." Or, "Follow, but beware impeding."

Or perhaps the assault from on high is related to guilt, and necessary consequence? Moses has killed; shall he walk free?

Yes, no. With this god, one had best prepare for shock. Moses too had best prepare.

Prepare, to be surprised—a contradiction in terms? It would appear so. Moses is solemnly summoned. Vis-à-vis, he must deal with the god. Shake in your sandals; and on occasion, remove them.

Prepare, be astonished. The instruction barely holds together, it is rife with inner contradictions. Fruitful nonetheless.

~

> Through sacrificial rituals, acts normally unthinkable become possible. Sacrificial language serves to sanitize and sacralize the horror of atrocities, making them acceptable, if not always respectable . . .
>
> Sacrificial rituals and mindsets enable participants to displace responsibility for their actions onto a higher power, abdicating their own responsibility, often in the name of obedience. Because we are sacrificing in a holy cause, we can maintain the myth of innocence in relation to our own behavior . . .[11]
>
> —*Mary Condren, in* Concilium

~

The law of the Fall. Centuries of violence rend the tribes of earth, rend humans from their gods as well. Such a time must come and go and inevitably come again. Humans must shed blood, and taste blood, and turn the creation crimson with their deeds. Must; what we must. This is the dire edict of the Realm of Necessity.

Only gradually, and with what pain and loss, will we come to know a truth long hidden. To know that our God is of a different mind, hand raised in a different gesture than the Fury that descended on Moses. A gesture of blessing.

And in virtue of that blessing, we may come to know another way than that of murder, whether sanctioned or paid for.

Exodus 4–10

EXODUS 4

Verse 27 and following

First things first—a reunion with brother, Aaron, then with the elders. And again, one notes with admiration the economy of words and gestures. Get on with the story and its tasks!

Moses is emerging from shadow and shame. No longer the hunted criminal, the slave among slaves, twice exiled. He is set afire, a human torch lit from a desert bush.

The author would have us miss nothing. Prodigious signs are promised, to be worked through the simple gesture of a hand or a shepherd's crook.

(And never again, be it added, shall there occur a nocturnal assault by an impenetrable, nameless Fury!)

Moses stands free, marked with his credential of blood, the first of the circumcised. And among his own he is transformed, a vizier.

~

It is as though we are in a darkened theatre, with great events in the offing; the curtain is closed, but it billows out in a gale of portent, the thunder and lightning of a Sophoclean or Shakespearean drama.

Then, to blinding light, the curtain opens. The conductor appears, moves with dignity to the apron of the stage. He raises his arms—the baton holds steady. He and his musicians will accompany and interpret the grand events shortly to unfold. And be it known that he is not only conductor—he composes the music as well.

~

On stage are the protagonists, Moses and Aaron. We note the deportment: audacious, unsubdued, as the brothers approach the throne of the sun king. In defiance of custom, they stand erect before him.

Will they bow and scrape? They will not. The scene is in utter defiance of courtesy or rubric. It implies a not so covert royal deflation.

Consider their status in the world. Was not the elder, Moses, all but disposed of in infancy? And in adulthood was he not stigmatized, a murderer?

Further, is the immortal one to be thought so easily accessible—and to nonentities such as these? The friezes of the era serve as great instructors in matters of court etiquette. Custom is set in stone. Rulers are olympians; slaves are less than human. Often slaves are portrayed as diminished to half size, or less. They crouch in corvée under the whip, or kneel like human footstools before the throne. And should the majesty pass by, even at distance, these must bow and scrape and avert their eyes.

~

The pharaoh decides to hear the two out. In the way of his kind, he judges cannily. The brothers are potential troublemakers. Grant them audience then, if only to learn what matters are buzzing among the slaves.

Thus the all-but-unthinkable scene and its inner dynamic—on both sides. In the brothers, no fear and trembling, no protocol observed; we read of no request for an appointment.

Moses and Aaron, a kind of Walt Whitman pair. Free and easy, democratic, leveling, brash, they enter the royal presence and stand there. It is as though the pharaoh were reduced to a kind of foreman, a laborer draped in a leather apron, overseeing some public work or other. Could not so minor an entity be easily approached?

Unconscionable, impudent! They will deal with him as his equals. He is seated, as befits. Their stance implies an equable spirit, a slight concession to his dignity—allow him his throne, why not? Equality, inequality, what matter? The future belongs to us.

~

For a time the three converse quietly. They are testing the waters, taking measure of the adversary. Then the talk hottens up. They dicker, argue, mollify, grow red in the face; one party or another departs in dudgeon, returns for another round.

Our text is hardly to be accounted an official court record. It is biblical history "from below," with a vengeance.

The magniloquent one, the sun god? He is reduced, exiguous; he fades before our eyes. Nothing in official art or annals of the period prepares us for this subtle, unmistakable deflation.

Only this is required of biblical folk. That they be steadfast in vocation, speaking and living the truth.

~

Talk about reversal of roles! Heroic types emerge, these brothers. Officially they are slaves; that is the verdict from above. But in their own yes, and in the eyes of multitudes, "refuseniks," so to speak. Assured, foursquare and free, in service to Another, an immeasurably Greater.

And what of the pharaoh and his behavior? A chameleon king, a creature of moods. He morphs to fox or mule as occasion dictates; a mind quick but pinched, a narrow eye, a wizened heart. He bargains and reneges, cuts corners, equivocates, yields under pressure, then betrays his sworn word.

A moral portrait? One imagines a carven monument commemorating these days of wrath and nimble wits. The pharaoh would be diminished, a slave, a footstool for the easement of invincible purpose. And the brothers towering above.

~

Various meetings follow, inconclusively. The demands of Moses and Aaron vary; voices, sometimes dissident, sometimes complementary, are heard.

We are puzzled, on the track of "different traditions." The text mirrors the events; it is often clumsy and inconclusive. Deliberately so, one thinks. Jumbled and tumbled, the style is subtly instructive as worldly powers flounder about, in crisis.

The pharaoh, as has been suggested, is a type. A telling stroke has been suggested; he bears no name. To name him would be to blunt the sharp point. His kind behaves thus; they construct labyrinths, lead the vulnerable down nightmarish corridors, leading nowhere, into lies, equivocations, threats, pledges broken.

~

And many, though forewarned, adopt the pharaonic game. They play and deceive and are deceived. They harden and become bearers of tawdry, false hopes.

~

Let us imagine for a moment that the brothers yield before this autonomous, bruising nonentity—that, worn by interminable contention, they had compromise. Suppose that small gains accrue. The burden of slavery is somewhat relieved, straw is once more supplied for brick making, the workers' food allowance is doubled, that zestful Egyptian menu of steaming fleshpots . . .

Why not yield? Did our ancestors not endure the ills we fret over, and worse? Are we better, stronger than they?

And let us, the players, be realistic! Suppose the pharaoh allows us to depart. Wilderness, scorching sun, minimal food, scant water, wild beasts lurking. And what prospect, all said, of arrival in a better land?

~

Let us suppose (as actually occurs) that the request of the enslaved is a simple one—that the Hebrews be allowed a "three days sojourn into the desert," there to offer sacrifice to the newly revealed Yahweh. Shall Moses and Aaron settle for this?

According to one version, this is the actual stipulation, pared to the bone.

And it meets with distemper and denial. Permission denied!

Patrician nose to the wind, the pharaoh senses victory in the offing. Less is demanded; I will refuse even that. No budging; I have pushed these two against a wall!

Royal thumbs turn emphatically down. Three days? Intolerable! How then will fare his works and pomps, standing unfinished at the whim of ne'er-do-wells? His brows contract. He senses a ruse. What they seek, truth told, is relief from labor, idleness.

~

A far different demand is also recorded. It is incomparably vaster than the other—by eons, by cosmic implication. It turns a slavish existence on its head, offering for ages to come, dramatic symbols of a doughty, imaginative quest, a holy grail leading on. This. "Let My people go!"

Cut the bonds. Cancel the hopeless history. Set us free, once for all. At our own pace, in our own direction, under our own aegis. Let us shake the dust of Egypt from our sandals, the shameful memories—centuries of shame.

This is no servile, diminished request, no bargain struck in dim prospect of a more benign tyranny. Once for all, strike the chains!

~

The brothers stand before the pharaoh. Their faces are stony with purpose. A nimbus burns about their heads, visible to the inner eye. Pharaoh beware! These are the first freed slaves; they have freed themselves from tyrannous destiny, from hopelessness.

Their stance, the demands they push against odds—these are proof of the marvel. It will come. To them, it has already come.

Dangerous. These two are dangerous. Pharaoh: wheel, deal with care.

It is as though a trip-hammer were raised; the stroke falls. In the imperial mirror, where reality had heretofore seemed flawlessly platonic, time fuses with eternity. And the mirror explodes.

Now, what does great pharaoh see? A filigreed web of fragments, a vast realm gone to rubble, breakage beyond repair. The millennial self-image of the dynasty is shattered.

~

Oppression, it would seem, is like the moss and unavoidable. . . .
The compassion of the oppressed for the oppressed is indispensable. . . .
It is the world's one hope.[12]

—*Bertolt Brecht*

~

Can one summon an auditory analogue of such events, perhaps the perma-scream of a Munch painting or the portrait of a prince of the church by Francis Bacon? The soul's mutilation stands plain; the face falls away;

the pigment liquefies; down the canvas drips a runnel of ruin. It is as though hellfire within were dissolving the condemned into a bloody pottage, past all recognition.

~

"My people" must go. A greater than the pharaoh (than whom on earth there is no greater), has spoken. A greater in heaven, a voice audible on earth.

We have heard it before in scripture, the fall of a tyrant:

Suddenly opposite the lampstand, the fingers of a human hand appeared, writing on the plaster of the wall in the king's palace . . .
Then Daniel was brought into the presence of the king . . .
This is the writing that was inscribed: *Mene Tekel Peres.*
Mene, God has numbered your kingdom and put an end to it.
Tekel, you have been weighed in the scales and found wanting.
Peres, your kingdom has been divided . . . (Dan 5:5; 5:13; 5:25–28)

~

It is an old biblical theme: the toppling of thrones. The Christian scripture as well celebrates the event:

After this, I saw another angel come down from heaven, with great authority given him.

The earth was lit up with his glory. At the top of his voice, he shouted:

"Babylon has fallen, Babylon the great has fallen, has become the haunt of devils and a lodging for every foul spirit and loathsome bird . . ." (Rev 18:1–2)

~

The pharaoh is judged and found wanting. Let him fume and fumble about, dissembling, delaying. It is all up with him and his noxious system.

The event is not so simple as a departure, into heat and drought and desert sun, of a tribe of troublesome slaves. These Hebrews are after all expendable, replaceable in the next military skirmish or law-and-order roundup.

But that announcement, that judgment, who would not quail? A trumpet blast!

This occurs. A new God has entered the world, an epiphany. He stands over against the Egyptian pantheon and its votaries, nullifying them.

≈

And one's spirit quails too, even though far removed in time and dignity from the pharaoh, even as he fails and pales. Failure of nerve, of that adamant confidence, assuring in the invincible voice of the bloodline: I, only I am in command.

"Fool," the gospel names him. Let him know; he inhabits the palace of a single day; a shack thrown together from sand and shingle. And the sea is rising in a great wind.

One longs for this centuries later: to summon the artful insolence of the brothers, as they stride toward the throne and nail the pharaoh with a glance!

≈

The star of Moses is ascending. He awaits the hammer of Michelangelo, creating a marmoreal giant, his beard wild as a nest of serpents, his head horned, alight with the fires of Sinai.

Then one remembers, and the memory plants one's feet on terra firma once more. Moses killed, and escaped retribution. But not entirely: by a hair's breadth. Once, as he was on the road from exile, the deity sought to kill him.

But now, dangerous spasms are done with. Forgiven or forgotten or both, by Yahweh, by the pharaoh, is—the murder and flight of the hero.

One is well advised to forgive. And one refuses to forget. Thus perhaps daring to amend, even to rebuke the text. As the text itself by implication seems to invite second, better thoughts.

≈

EXODUS 5

Promises made, promises broken. There opens a wearying series of meetings, the sage of the iron pharaoh and the Brothers Adamant.

Matters are stalled, at impasse. And the god of Moses hovers near, alive with jealousy, an invisible prompter at the ear of his favorites.

An earthly sovereign is the adversary, in contention with mere slaves. Mere? Granted, but slaves teamed with a heavenly protagonist. Can the outcome be in doubt?

Still, attention is on edge. Under feverish stress, the stakes rise and rise.

~

The first demand is laid down; we have heard it before.

Flatly put, a feeler? The brothers ask for three days' freedom. Let the people depart and offer sacrifice in the desert.

Is this the premise—that the people go forth with every intention of returning—to submission, chains and labor? A collective respite and no more, a breathing space, worship of Yahweh at distance from the offending idols?

Even under so shaky a premise, the pharaoh is well advised, in accordance with imperial logic, to turn thumbs down. By no means!

These people are unsubdued by forty-five generations of corvée. Is it to be imagined that, granted a modicum of freedom, they will return to lockup, to a human cattle pen? Pharaohs are no fools; empires do not flourish on follies or phantasies. Let the pharaoh be wary, summon resolute purpose, nip these opportunists in bud.

~

A counterstroke, a preemptive blow is called for. "That same day" the infamous order is issued to the Egyptian and Hebrew overseers. Thus, the same quota of bricks as before. And from henceforth, no straw is provided.

Bricks without straw! The first recorded catch-22 of imperial history—and hardly to be thought the last.

~

But wait. A straw, the adage goes, once broke the camel's back. The trope is apropos, the back in question being not the spine of slaves but (horrors!) the royal spine itself, stiff as the rod of Moses.

The order is harsh, impossible to fulfill. It could not but recoil and strike its author, a tactical boomerang, a reverse shock of humiliation and defeat. The scene that follows is like a children's charade, brutally direct, stripped down.

The "scribes" (strangely so named), Hebrew overseers, are universally despised, despised by their Egyptian masters, by the pharaoh who contemns them even as he finds them useful—and most fervently of all, by their own people.

The edict brings a further humiliation of these turncoats. Slave masters in a minor mode, must they now wield the whip ever more ruthlessly?

They must. They flail about, the backs and buttocks of slaves burn under the stripes. All to no avail. Production falls short.

Someone must be blamed, for sure. Why not these scribes? In a ladder-and-rung system, every master is a slave to the one above. The scribes, being Hebrew, have as masters Egyptian overseers. Who proceed to apply the bastinado with unholy ardor.

Like whipped dogs, the scribes limp to the pharaoh in search of relief. He hears them out, then with a wave of the hand, turns aside.

Shortly, Moses and Aaron encounter the dispirited rejects and are all but drowned in a torrent of reproach. Curious is the plaint of the sad apparatchiks, not a whisper of concern for the sufferings of their people. They whine like born underlings:

"You have brought us into bad odor with pharaoh and his court. You have put a sword in their hand to slay us."

~

We have noted before, each episode is relentlessly single-minded. Yahweh has intruded on the human scene, naming himself to his favorite, promising interventions that will challenge the empire to a showdown.

From the start the role of the deity is clear as high noon. In pursuit of the exodus event, this supernal one, advocate of slaves, will stand in combat with the pharaoh.

In a moment, like a celestial Sampson, the God will shake the foundations.

~

Central to the divine polity and event and motive is the question of means and ends. To the vast project, the god will bring a supreme weight of arm and mind, exerting himself to the utmost, even murderously, to save. To this end any means, it appears, will do.

"Thou shall not kill." Does the edict stand? And if it is said to stand firm, how comes the god to choose as his earthly collaborator an admitted murderer?

"Thou shall not kill." Dare we venture that the god becomes a scandal, jettisoning the command he [*sic*] has strenuously urged on humankind?

Urged, be it noted, through the mediation of the same Moses, a murderer.

And yet again, "Thou shall not kill." But does not violent death await the Egyptian innocents, victims of the first Passing Over? And who is the agent of the slaughter, if not a deity turned Herodian?

~

Let this be ventured as a law of biblical communality. In combat with the worst, the deity comes to resemble the worst. Morality is held hostage. In the Egyptian standoff, the cruelty of the god will mime that of his mortal adversary, the pharaoh.

The divine cruelty will surpass likewise his chosen, somewhat tainted favorite. Thus are our gods (or our god) often begotten in our image. To the demeaning of both parties.

~

Such reflections, one hastens to add, are not lightly set down. The text would seem to demand them. This Yahweh of Genesis and Exodus is a "jealous God." He longs to be loved—but in peculiar fashion, confusing as he frequently does, the stipulated "sacrifice in the desert," with love itself.

~

And what of our author of Exodus? To narrow the case, he can hardly be thought to love his God. Too cool for that is the text. Let us say, rather, he holds the deity in guarded respect. He reminds one of King Solomon, who kept lions in his gardens and warily, warily fed them by hand. And at feeding time was careful to station nearby, servants with swords drawn.

~

EXODUS 6

Moses, interceding, takes to Yahweh the plaints of the whipped scribes. Notably, neither the intercessor nor his divine patron appears angered by the malfeasance of the turncoats. No question is raised as to corporate punishment—whether, for instance, stripes might be thought fitting. No, goes the reasoning, these near nonentities are not the adversary; their peccadilloes are beneath serious note.

~

Pharaoh, that improbable, reneging absolute monarch, digs in his heels. And the great maned Lion in the sky positively roars with frustration and threat!
Yahweh:

You
shall see,
and shortly,

how I
shall deal

with
pharaoh.

Not only
will he

allow
my people
egress;

he
will force

them
out! (Exod 6:1)

~

Means to an end: sound end, dubious means? We have the divine dilemma taking a familiar, all-too-human form. And speedily too; the
means, both good and bad, are devised and shunted about, fore and aft,
bewilderingly. Poor author, one thinks, caught in his own toils! Tactics
are pernicious, invasive, worming their way into the soul. Into the soul of
Yahweh? Yahweh, captive of dark means?

Shall one go further and suggest that Yahweh and pharaoh seem at
times mirror images one of the other?

~

Further, take it further. The genius of the text allows no moralizing. Let
the story speak for itself. And a question: those means, tawdry, furtive,
morbid by turn: do they fail to entice the powerful? They do not fail; again
and again they enact the original sin seeded in the soul of the pharaohs of
earth. Dragon's teeth that beget warriors.

The hint of dubious means is imbedded in the promise, as the god
details his purpose. Success shall be mine! My people shall go out! He
takes, so to speak, the l o n g , l o n g view.

The exodus, the eventual arrival in the land of promise—these assured, what then? In strikingly brutal (pharaonic?) fashion, the deity will
clear Canaan of the unsuitable and unchosen, in favor of the inscrutably
chosen:

"I have decided to lead you up . . . into the land of the Canaanites,
Hittites, Amorites, Perizzites, Hivites and Jebusites . . ." (Exod 3:17)

~

Who shall live, and who die? And by what entitlement, grace or disgrace,
do such decrees fall? Is it godly to play god in this fashion? If freedom is
to be won at such cost, what is to be accounted gain? If wicked means are
socialized, then transmitted into the future, to lay a hand on institutions,

economies, the military, on conscience itself—what gain? If this is the god to be served, in denial of all others—what gain?

The questions are impertinent, inadmissible. For that, they must be raised. The text invites them. Embrace the oxymoron. "Prepare to be astonished" . . . And not only by the god.

~

EXODUS 7

Yahweh says it plain. Announcement: he himself will

> make
> the pharaoh
>
> so
> obstinate,
>
> that
> despite
>
> the many
> signs & wonders
>
> that I
> will work . . .
>
> he
> will not
>
> listen
> to
> you. (Exod 7:3–4)

And the purpose, as the lava-like heart of the pharaoh cools and turns stony?

> So that

the Egyptians

may
know

that I
am
God. (Exod 7:5)

In human terms, a bizarre mental construct, one thinks. Still, our author leaves it at that.

How not leave it at that? In principle the "plan" is beyond critique, issuing as it does from the bosom of all being.

∽

Someone named Jesus, however, lurks like a lion in the path of the future. His prey, so to speak, is the plan. His life and death will mount a shocking rebuke to our text and its serpent's tangle of means and ends. Implying (better, stating plain, in a script of blood), that The Plan falls far short of the divine.

Which is to say, far short of the human. Tyrannical, typical of the powers of this world. Hardly to be accounted blessed. Truth told, The Plan is—pharaonic.

∽

Moses and Aaron, it develops, are shortly to be endowed with quasi-divine powers. Their shepherd's crook will wave about in the air; wonders will proliferate, surpassing the powers of the vizards of Egypt. And eventually this redoubtable duet will constrain the pharaoh to bow before the divine will.

∽

The magic of Moses and his brother, as matters turn, proves seductive, surpassing. The marvels wrought have passed into the folklore of the tribe, like the passing of a wizard's crook, hand to hand, generation to generation. The book of Wisdom (11:14–20; 16:1–18) offers a spectacular midrash on these episodes. And two lengthy psalms (Psalm 78 and Psalm 105), for a total of 117 verses, celebrate the fraternal wonders.

Perhaps in this vast elaboration, the Bible has taken the Bible too seriously? We are permitted, perhaps even advised, to remain somewhat short of transfixed—bemused perhaps by the competing hocus pocus. It all seems somewhat tawdry, a circus befitting Egyptian magians rather than the deity and his prophet-brothers.

Or perhaps relief is the point. The tone of the stories is ironic, subtly (or not so subtly) deflating, to those who walk the pages—magians, pharaoh, brothers, gods—and yes, the god.

Could he be implying, this author and his subtleties, this: a pox on all your houses? This: you believers, look further, deeper for truth, for religion, for true God?

~

> The first thing we can say about faith's imagination is that it composes reality with irony and with ironic images.
> . . . [I]rony deals not with appearances, but with the very opposite of appearances . . . [I]ts main task is to keep opposites together in a single act of the imagination. Thus if we ask the question, what is power? Who has the real power? Appearance will say that the powerful have power, but the beatitudes and the sermon on the mount in the Gospel of St. Matthew say the opposite. Like the imagination itself, faith moves below appearances into existence. In the primary sense of the word *metaphysical* they are both metaphysical.[13]
>
> —*William F. Lynch, SJ*

~

It is lengthily announced like the riff of a skilled trumpet, this contest of the god vs. the gods.

And we are led to question, on whose terms? It is as though the deity consents to sup with the devil but neglects to carry a long spoon. Or as though the opening scene of the book of Job were being enacted again: Yahweh vs. the Satan. Here as there, a notable trickster faces off with the god.

We take note; it is as though the god were to enter the contest blind-folded and thereupon were spun about, dizzy.

Here too, in the rules of the game, as well as in the various wonders to be wrought, one cannot but note that the Egyptians seize the initiative.

How comes this? Step by step the god will be forced into an Egyptian corner where lurk the principalities named moral ambiguity and death. And finally the god of Moses will stand before a distorting mirror, issuing a mandate that can only be termed murderously pharaonic. Let the children die!

What difference, all said, between the two Faustian decrees, between the death of Hebrew male infants and the death of Egyptian first born? Are we to abominate the former, and celebrate the latter? The mind boggles.

~

Will the deity come on no better way of manifesting the power of truth? He [sic] will, and that way will have its epiphany. But only centuries later. The law is adamant. Centuries must pass; we humans are ruinously slow learners; we mime the worst, ignoring or persecuting the precious and best among us.

Then a breakthrough. At long last our hearts will be warmed and ourselves won over. And this, be it noted, through no spectacle or contest of power. Quite the opposite: by the modesty of Christ, his human measure, his renunciation of every form of the Promethean and magical.

~

But we anticipate. Back to our Contest of Marvels. Pharaoh, the brothers, the clutch of Egyptian magians. Lo! a gesture, and the wand of Moses is transformed to a serpent (or whatever, a dragon or crocodile, the accounts vary wonderfully).

Comes the turn of the local magians, a fraternity of "Jannes and Jambres." They too wave wands about. And a second Lo! and a like transmogrification.

Then the loudest Lo! of all. The serpent (or whatever fauna) of Moses, larger by supposition and more voracious by far, swallows whole the opponents' whatever!

~

One is meant perhaps to recall here subtle reference to a primordial serpent, that wreaker of havoc (Genesis 3).

And one day, the prophet Ezekiel will deride great pharaoh, a "crocodile," in an extended image of carnivorous ferocity (Ezekiel 32).

~

For his part, the pharaoh remains unimpressed by the Mosaic marvels. Or, perhaps more accurately, remains obdurate. And his mulish willfulness is noted on high, frowningly.

But wait, the pharaoh shall be turned round; Yahweh has further marvels, one almost said, "up his sleeve." Blood. The waters of Egypt, in "streams and canals and pools," even in "wood buckets and stone jars" (such detailed, vivid enumeration)—all are turned to blood.

"There was blood everywhere in Egypt." The image is awful—and accurate. The feat of Moses will be fearfully verified, dramatized throughout the empire. First in wars, then in an edict, the firstborn of the Hebrews must die.

~

The Plague of Blood

("Blood everywhere," and not only in Egypt. In the aftermath of the exodus, wars of conquest bring the promise to an altogether ambiguous outcome. The empire emerges in the era of Solomon. Now wars are waged for a different purpose: expansion of borders and foreign markets. War becomes the health of the superstate.)

The law of the Fall is verified, embodied, ensanguined in the horrid feat of Moses. All turns to blood—for all turn to bloodshed.

~

And our sanguinary appetite is assuaged with a healing elixir:

My
Blood,

shed
for

you. (Matt 26:28)

∽

Assuaged, our sanguinary appetite? In the twentieth century of carnage just past, dare one set the words down?

Let us amend them. At least this—the shedding of blood is discredited by the gift of Jesus: "My blood, shed for you." The "just war" fabrications are unmasked. Death is undone, and by the hardest of means—the undergoing of death.

∽

> We have NATO in the sky and the tyrant on the ground and we are being crushed.[14]
>
> —*Kosovo, "Women in Black"*

∽

> In 1919, Gandhi confessed that he had overestimated his followers' understanding of and capacity for nonviolence, calling it a "Himalayan miscalculation."
>
> Maybe. But our Himalayan miscalculation seems to go in the other direction; we seem to overlook repeatedly the capacity for nonviolence and the people who are brave enough to try it in the face of overwhelming hatred.
>
> That is what has to change if we are to see peace in the next millennium.[15]
>
> —*Michael Nagler, American scholar and activist*

∽

Our pharaonic drama languishes in stalemate. As though a Greek tragedy were in progress, we see the obdurate ruler turning away; with a deep frown he enters "into his house," with no concern even for this, this rubric laid on the land, a red mist that covers all.

In the "seven days" that bring no relief, does the pharaoh drink blood or bathe in blood?

~

The Plague of Frogs

Of these beasts and their infestation it appears that the pharaoh shortly has had enough, and more. A royal pattern of behavior is set; in anticipation of relief, stony purpose yields;

"Remove the frogs, and I will let the people go."

Relief, review, then reneging. The frogs die off, the slaves toil on.

~

Verses 16 and following

The Plague of Gnats

The dust of the earth comes alive with the wee beasties, people and animals their prey. We are not told whether the affliction touches on the Hebrews.

And for the first time, the necromancers of Egypt come up short; they cannot produce so much (or so little) as a single gnat. And for the first time, the magians are impelled to a remarkable confession before pharaoh: "the finger of God is here" (Exod 8:19).

Defeat, faith, both?

~

It is by the "finger of God" that Jesus will exorcise the demons (Luke 11:20; Matt 12:28). By the same power, he adds: "the Reign of God is upon you."

And we have in the hymn "Veni Creator," a like image of the Holy Spirit; *digitus paternae dexterae*: "finger of the Father's right hand . . ."

~

Nothing avails to turn the tyrant about, neither the failure of his magians nor their spectacular confession.

~

Verses 20 and following

The Plague of Flies

So, yet another visitation: flies, multiplying everywhere. For the first time, purportedly, exception is made; no swarms afflict the Hebrews.

And, *eccolo*, the pharaoh is willing to strike a bargain; the people of Moses may offer sacrifice but only in Egypt! Compromise within compromise, and by no means agreeable. Moses must explain the Hebrew objection—which would appear obvious. (Perhaps the explanation is a kind of archeological footnote for sake of an uninformed posterity? The beasts immolated in Hebrew ritual were sacred to the Egyptians. One people's sacrifice, another's sacrilege!)

Moses shifts his strategy. "In effect, my people must depart the land, lest they be stoned by the outraged Egyptians."

"Very well then," avers volatile Pharaoh. "You may go, but not too far away." And (all unexpectedly) "Pray for me."

Is Pharaoh more complex than we thought? Or more canny, stealing a march, a fake attitude, from his chastened magic men?

~

Moses is forthright. He raps the royal knuckles. *Pharaoh must cease playing false with us, refusing to let my people go!* The exchange is like a children's story. And charming too; the royal heart is not altogether of hewn stone, and a valiant spirit summons the king to accounts.

A heart not altogether of stone. But still unyielding. The request is denied: "Thou shalt not go."

~

EXODUS 9

Verse 1 and following

From serious affliction to more serious still, the ecological cost mounts. A pestilence strikes domestic beasts, the animals scorched by the burning eye of Yahweh. And the cattle of the Hebrews are adroitly separated out; no misfortune falls to them!

It is as though our author revels in the fact. The pharaoh makes careful inquiry, finding—to his undoubted dismay—not a single beast of the Hebrews has perished! Nonetheless, no budging.

~

Do we have here an extended parable, suggesting that misfortune seldom brings a change of heart—especially the heart of a king and his kind? Ours is a drama of willful authority under duress, a tyrant stuck in tyranny, unyielding.

The pharaoh is heavily afflicted. And he turns and turns about. Promises, promises are solemnly sworn. Then with feral ease, all is forsworn.

In the Christian scripture, too, a warning. A plague of obduracy afflicts others than the pharaohs of the world.

The rest of the human race, who escaped these plagues, refused to stop worshiping devils—or to abandon the things they had made with their own hands, the idols made of gold, silver, bronze, stone and wood, that can neither see nor hear nor move.

> Nor did they give up their murdering or witchcraft, or fornication or stealing. (Rev 9:20–21)

~

The parable of the people vs. the pharaoh (if our text be taken as such) is set down like all of scripture, "for our instruction." We are invited to take a close and critical look—one thinks a properly biblical look—at a like realpolitik flourishing in our lifetime.

A drama, as U.S. rulers follow one on another, this political party or that. They differ in no issue worth noting. Promises? These proliferate like flies or gnats or frogs or pestilence—or the turning of the waters of earth to blood. And the military establishment, bloated beyond measure or relief, is immune, off bounds to critique.

> For a decade or more, I have spoken and written of life under the bomb. I thought of it this way; as an "either-or": either the prospect of nuclear war threatening, or the reality of radioactive poison spewed globally from every stage of nuclear adventurism. I imagined an obtuse, hellish race between the immanence of nuclear war and death from radioactive toxins. I imagined a kind of suicidal choice placed before us humans: quick or slow "omnicide."

However, such categories are not finally useful. Our relationship with the bomb is not an either-or, not war or poison. It is
both.[16]

—*Philip Berrigan, from prison, 2000*

~

No matter who holds the reins of American power, the behavior (i.e.,
cynicism, greed, clash of arms, contempt for the poor) stands deep set
in place. The people are betrayed, legitimate needs are unmet, the ecol-
ogy languishes, freedom is honored in petrifying clichés and denied in
practice.

And war, that monstrous mantra, is matter-of-factly invoked: always,
recourse to war. Once more, in the autumn of 2001, a flotilla of ruin sets
out for Afghanistan and Iraq. Purpose: bloodletting, vengeance.

~

Verse 8 and following

The Plague of Boils

Back to our storied contest. In the presence of the pharaoh, the brothers
stoop and gather up handfuls of soot, fling them in a cloud skyward. The
cloud settles; ulcers erupt on the bodies of the Egyptians. (The event is
conveyed in the word *sehin*, also describing the affliction of Job).

And a detail; the magians are helpless to duplicate the dark feat. And
worse befalls; they are so afflicted as to be 'unable to stand before the
king.'

Neither, one thinks, will the king long stand before Moses; nor for
that matter, will he sit secure on his throne.

~

No budging. Yahweh has hardened the heart of the pharaoh.

This attribution to the god of a heart turned stony is often "ex-
plained" somewhat dismissively, as "a Hebraism." The harsh expression,
we are told, can be understood through a series of mediating "secondary
causes" or by recourse to a so-called permissive will of Yahweh.

But what if one were to take the expression at face value?

Paul it would seem, does so:

God
has mercy

on whom
he [*sic*] wishes,
and
whom

he wishes,

he
makes
obdurate. (Rom 9:18)

—and this in reference to our present text!

In agreement with the Pauline hypothesis, the Yahweh-Pharaoh crisis is wonderfully heightened. And the character of Yahweh, like a sunstruck jewel, shows yet another facet, blinding and baffling. Paul again:

Scripture says to pharaoh—

This
is why
I
raised you up;
that through you
I might show
my power,

and my name
be
proclaimed

throughout
the
earth. (Rom 9:17).

~

A "best case" might go somewhat like this: the god in a sense steps aside. Thereupon the powerful pluck off their masks and wreak their worst. And all to (eventual) good. The virtue of such as Moses and multitudes of the faithful shines the brighter; so does the glory of Yahweh, age upon age.

~

Verse 13 and following

The Plague of Hail

Hail, lightning, fierce storms. Wonderfully vivid, the account. And divine logic is relentless, rampageous even, rife with ego. Thus; I could have wiped you all from the face of the earth. But no. According to Paul, mercy prevailed:

> This
> is why
>
> I
> spared you
>
> that my name
> be known
>
> throughout
> the
> earth. (Rom 9:17, quoting Exod 9:16)

With due respect for Paul, still, one thinks, the "power" he commends is ambiguous, shot through with a spirit of vengeance.

~

Verses 24 and 26

"Thunder, hail and fire." And the "land of Goshen, where the sons of Israel were" is again exempt.

But the Egyptians, what of them? Anonymous subjects of a lord who makes of them accomplices and clones and yes, slaves; these must suffer for the sins of their ruler.

~

One thinks of a parallel; a decade of shame, sanctions wickedly enforced against Iraq, in despite of compassion or human feeling. The withholding of medical supplies and food killed multitudes of children—and this under pretext of punishing their (presumably wicked) leader.

~

Here it is Yahweh, we are told, who pummels the multitudes with ecological disaster. The offense is personal, the punishment socialized. What a god is set before us!

And the pharaoh, by turns bumptious and groveling, confesses sin—and sins the more. A kind of showcase tyrant, and a livid warning as well: the consequence of violating the human measure.

~

And for that matter, what of Moses, canny and devious, powerful of mien and gesture—and long in unprevailing? He reads the crooked heart of Pharaoh and his ilk. The mood is darkly clairvoyant:

I know
you

and
your counselors

do
not

as
yet

fear
god. (Exod 9:30)

~

It is perhaps meant as irony. Let us even dare suggest—it is meant as an irony that fails. The incompatibles, the contraries are there and held in considerable tension. (*Will the pharaoh yield? Will my people be let go?*) But the lofty one, Yahweh, and the lowly, the pharaoh, are unevenly matched in resources and stealth and purpose. The elaborate scaffolding falls; the ridiculous overwhelms the sublime.

It is meant to; our author is a magian, an authentic one. We take note of the subversive glint in his eye. He means to undermine conventional expectation; literally, to "mime from beneath." In order that eventually, and after unutterable travail, hope in a truer God might emerge.

Let brows wrinkle in perplexity. It is all "for our instruction," perpetually teasing the mind.

~

EXODUS 10

Verse 1 and following

The plague of locusts is introduced with a boast; even the dignity of choosing wickedly is withdrawn from the pharaoh. The deity speaks:

It is
I

who
have made him
obdurate,

in order that I
might perform
these wonders . . .

and that you
may recount

to son

and grandson

how

ruthlessly

I

dealt ... (Exod 10:1–2)

The "in order that," the double-purpose, pleads for underscoring. The sin of the pharaoh has for its source the omnipotence of Yahweh. But is not Yahweh a being who in principle is above sin? Not only that, but the tale is made glorious, peerless, immortal. It must be told and retold, the subject of generational folklore. Let it even issue in liturgies, in worship.

Bad faith puffing itself as good?

Further, the "mighty deeds" reveal precisely the nature of Yahweh:

that you
may know

who
is
Yahweh. (Exod 10:2)

∽

Do we have a purpose revealed, but in a way altogether unintended?

In light of our great midrash, the gospel of Jesus, we are given to know much concerning this Yahweh—and much that he is not.

One thinks of Oedipus striding confident, straight toward ruin. And guilt turns like a blade against his own body; he blinds himself. A sign.

∽

The Plague of Locusts

The threat befalls: locusts. The entire court is present. And once more the depredations-to-be are described in wondrously dire detail. To wit; whatever of living things remains intact after the hailstorms, voracious insects devour.

But wait. Some among those present have had enough of gloom and doom. They approach the pharaoh. The angry word spills out, *tout court*: enough!

And for once the tyrant softens; he hearkens to his own. Moses and Aaron are summoned and the dickering—feint, dodge, shuffle—resumes.

Now try this:

"Of course you may go. But exactly who are to go along with you?"

Answer: forthright. In effect,

"Everyone, young and old; and our herds and flocks as well. Yahweh's will is clear; a celebration must include all our clan and all available fauna!"

Subterfuge of course. And wily Pharaoh pounces.

The departure proposed is a sham. It is hardly to be thought the commencement of a worshipful three-day interlude. By no means! This is the real thing, a universal one-way exit, definitive.

Not to be. Permission withdrawn.

~

Come then, locusts, in clouds! And shortly the living landscape succumbs to scissoring jaws.

Yahweh too is busy, tightening the knotted will of pharaoh.

No breakthrough.

~

Verse 21 and following

The Plague of Darkness

Then the ninth plague, darkness. Shakespearean. "Night thickens." Dawn is canceled, and high noon and sunset. Three days—of utter night. (And who, we marvel, counts their passing, those fantastic days of night?)

The upshot: bargaining, bargaining once more. And a concession: the children may go; the beasts must stay put. A nice touch of casuistry. *How, pray, are a people to survive in a wilderness with no cattle for sustenance?* Moses is unfazed. He shifts the debate to a religious basis. (Neither side, we note, admits to the real issue: the survival of those who mean to depart, once for all).

Moses: the fact is plain. We must have the animals, every hoof and claw of them, for sacrifice to Yahweh. Then a fine-tuned note:

" . . . we will not know which ones to choose until we arrive at the place itself."

Pharaoh, walking a very tunnel of contingencies, stubborn as an Egyptian mule, is now furious as well.

> Go
> from here;
>
> if
> you appear
> again
>
> before me,
>
> you
> will
> die. (Exod 10:28)

And Moses, equable;

> You
> have said it.
>
> I
> shall
> never
>
> return
> here. (Exod 10:29)

Michael Ronall recalls a Seder that took place some forty years ago and involved the two children of family friends. Gabriel, six years old, asked Rachel, his fourteen-year-old sister, about the plagues that God caused the ancient Egyptians to suffer on behalf of the Israelites.

"I don't understand," Gabriel said. "I thought God was supposed to be good and kind and loving to people. How could he do such horrible things to the Egyptians?"

"You have to realize," Rachel replied. "God was very young at the time."[17]

—*Enid Nemy,* New York Times

~

EXODUS 11

We come at length to the ultimate test of wills: the tenth plague, the decree ordering the death of the firstborn of Egypt. As before, various traditions have their say, as does the overshadowing editor. He would have us know it beyond doubt; he takes the word in charge. Responsible and proud, he owns it.

And as matters grow sanguinary, he pushes in our faces the primal mover of events: Yahweh. What, we marvel, is the editorial purpose, setting down such sentiments as these?

Yahweh said to Moses, "The pharaoh will refuse to listen, so that my prodigious acts might be many in Egypt" (Exod 11:9).

And so on.

~

Does the author seek to awaken in us a sense of righteous pride in such a god—or a sense of shame? In either case, a few preliminary reflections would seem in order, indeed biblically required.

We have noted it before; often in Exodus, and later as well, the behavior of the god is qualified by his *[sic]* human connections. And this in quite striking ways. Dealing with kings and pharaohs, the deity takes on a worldly coloration, leans toward tendencies of the fallen authorities—power grubbing, war making, or (as here) outright murder of the innocent.

But. Only let the deity hearken to the saints, and (as we shall see) the tendency is strikingly otherwise. Friendship with heroic spirits transfigures; the god undergoes an epiphany of improved behavior. He pauses. Second thoughts arise concerning favorites. He grows merciful, clairvoyant, compassionate toward the victimized. Feminine urges sway his heart; the god incubates us as in a womb, becomes a materfamilias of humans. Images arise bespeaking mercy from on high. Through Isaiah the deity

> writes
> us
>
> in
> the palm
>
> of
> his
> hand. (Isa 49:16)

~

Likewise, grown prophetic through intimacy with Jeremiah, God promises a return, the end of catastrophe and exile. Summoning the gift, the Deity waxes ecstatic:

> The One
> who scattered
> Israel,

will
gather him

and
keep him

as a shepherd
keeps
his flock . . .

and they
shall be
radiant

over
the bounty
of God . . .

over the grain
and the new wine
and the oil . . .

and their life
shall be

like
a watered garden,

and they
shall never

languish
again . . . (Jer 31:10, 12)

~

Thus the human renewed induces a deity renewed. Destiny is transformed to vocation, in heaven as on earth. No more insiders for whose divine favor the outsiders must pay. Juridical scales reckoning to a featherweight our human worth or worthlessness—these are put aside once for all.

Henceforth it is the heart that matters, the sacred heart. That organ of love becomes, so to speak, the heart of transformation. A once-vexed, tempestuous, nearly ruinous matter (that is, the divine-human commerce) is renewed.

~

But we are trudging along the hard road of Exodus; we are nowhere near the Himalayan height of the eighth to fifth centuries BCE, the era of the prophets. We are, alas, in the era of Pharaoh versus an ambiguous god.

The decree promulgated by the pharaoh was overbearing, lapsarian, hostile to life, emptied of mercy. It demanded the death of Hebrew children. And the god is about to follow suit, bloody tit for tat. Kill the innocents, the newborn! Life in its first stirrings must be crushed.

The nadir approaches. Its prelude is an atmosphere that rolls past the "three days" of the ninth plague, thick with palpable darkness (Exod 10:22). Ironies awful, dislocating to good sense, proceed apace.

A decree of death, the death of Egyptian children, will resolve the divine-pharaonic impasse. The decree of Pharaoh was of earth, earthly. The second decree is purportedly of heaven and for that reason doubly awful. The first was issued by a regal "dweller on earth," the second from a god (dare we say a deity?) ethically assimilated to the same "dweller."

Truly, we have come full (and foul) circle.

~

The pharaoh's decree against the Hebrews was a matter of gross realpolitik: who shall live and who die. The awful decision was presented by our laconic storyteller to be quite uncomplicated by moral niceties.

Moralizing, it would seem, attenuates the text. The literary tone is unfailingly cool. Stirrings of rage or aversion are left to ourselves.

~

Pharaoh commanded all his subjects:

"Throw into the river every boy that is born to the Hebrews" (Exod 1:22).

In male numbers lurked the restive strength of a slave populace. So. The good estate of the empire demanded their "limitation," a useful, simple abstraction, reminiscent of lesser-evil casuists of a later time.

And what of the divine decree? It is trebly problematic in intent, execution, and redoubtable sanction. And no one to challenge, be it noted, no prophet barring the way. From Moses and Aaron not a sigh of resistance. In this matter of life and death, the brothers are little more than puppets animated by a supreme vocalizer.

~

Undoubtedly, the episode story places us in a dangerous corner, in the era of "religion of no challenge." Shall the god so act and no questions be raised? If so, the god will become a berserker.

~

A further difficulty: The Hebrews were protected from former plagues. The present decree, the death of Egyptian firstborn, also protects Hebrew children. But with what a difference! This decree of protection is not only sanctioned; it is also shortly to be made sacrosanct. It will be transformed in a rite known as the "paschal mystery," celebrating the long-sought, long-delayed triumph: the exodus from Egypt.

The immolation of the lamb is integrated with a symbolic offering of the Hebrew firstborn and a lifting up of the first fruits of harvest. A prescription, a "passover," a ritual of "passing over." Elevated to a liturgy, the decree is summarily removed from the arena of ethical debate or objection. The Hebrew exemption and the death of Egyptian children—these simply stand, sacrosanct for eons.

The two events are embedded in time as though in amber. Parents are to recount the story to the (Hebrew) children with all due reverence.

The rite demands submission, thanksgiving—as though in face of a holy intervention. True believers will gather and consume the lamb. Memories will grow fragrant and grateful.

But . . . but . . . Those memories! Pause; regard them closely.

They are inexorably tribal, implicitly cruel, accounting cheap the cost exacted from the "others," from innocents, from parents and siblings.

Must it always be the innocent who suffer, even at the hands of a god?

The pharaoh was hardly to be judged innocent. His decree: let the children pay. The vicious law continues in force to our day.

~

As I set down these notes, more than a decade of deadly sanctions against the Iraqis have remained in place. Many Americans have visited the stricken country; its hospitals, homes, and schools; have spoken with doctors, parents, dying children. The accounts are invariably the same: devastating. More than a million Iraqi children have perished.

And American authorities are adamant, turned to stone. A secretary of state, asked to comment on the deaths, countered the question with a look of official petrifaction; "For us," she averred, "the sanctions are worth the cost."

The cost? But who pays?

~

"Why is this night unlike all other nights?" the father of a Hebrew family is instructed to raise the question. Highly selective memory is at work. Darkness falls, the grand passage out of slavery is imminent. And our story is the only story, our children the only children.

The dead have no story.

Do dead children have a story to tell? If so, how are they to tell it, and to whom? To one another, in a conventicle of the dead?

One matter is clear. They shall not tell it at this hearth, in this doorway.

Our story alone matters. We Hebrews, together with our children, are the ones saved.

For that matter, how shall the mothers of the dead children speak for them? How shall the fathers, these fathers placed outside the text? The outcry of parents, their weeping, is forbidden to have a place.

And among those who ponder the text, century after century, rare indeed are those who will ask, where are those others, why are they invisible, inaudible? Do they wail into a void? Has God forgotten them?

~

The questions are out of order; they are excluded from the rubric of this night. The deity has rendered the Egyptian children expendable, invisible, inaudible. So, according to our author, has Moses.

~

Yet the text, as given here, raises a welter of questions. Why should some children die, and others be held precious? Who shall speak (since the god refuses to speak) on behalf of all children?

And a further question, also impertinent, inadmissible—and therefore properly biblical: shall the god emerge as godly, except there be someone to say nay to him? To say no child must die! Someone. A Job, an Isaiah, a Jeremiah?

~

We have noted it, the tardy emergence of a mature, questioning faith. For the Mosaic present (and for centuries to come), there exists no naysayer. Only these patriarchal metronomes.

These, and the priestly shadow lying heavy on the text. A hand is armed with a knife. The supposition leaps ahead, then falls—a murderous mandate.

A preeminent mercy (and by implication, a preeminent mercilessness) is dramatized and passes into ritual. The tribe of ex-slaves is hereby charged with enactment of this memory: liberation for some, death for others.

Rejoice then, in the liberation.

Rejoice in the deaths? Say rather: Ignore "them, the others." This deity permits such "collateral damage."

Thus we are informed early on that the god takes sides. And more: that he personally intervenes, the original Angel of Extermination, in the awful tenth episode of a momentous stalemate.

And the deity would have his taking of sides memorialized, year after year, century after century. Let the taking of sides be mutual, a matter of heaven and earth renewing and solidifying a pact of advantage, a covenant binding humans (some humans) to the god. He has chosen; the choice stands firm. Let the chosen remember, and be grateful.

≈

By the same token and the same rite, let them keep alive the memory of enemies. From the first days of the tribe, there have been enemies. Now it is decreed, in effect, there will always be enemies. The assurance is compact with the sacrifice. Let the lamb be slain, the enemy confounded!

Thus, too, the future is rendered bleak, as the past was bleak.

The chosen were liberated, in a manner of speaking. But what of those prior inhabitants of the land of Promise, the tribes of Canaan? They are cast in the image of enemy. They, too, will be dealt with.

≈

The intervention in Egypt, and on and on through the desert years and the crossing of the Jordan—what choices, what cost! A cost exacted not only of the victims; of the victors also—and of their vindicating, sanguinary god.

One way of calculating the cost: the god and people are stuck with one another. Millennially, our ancestry is stuck. The warrior-god is wedded to a people of blood. Each manifestly approving the other (each deserving the other?).

What of another possibility, a nonviolent god, a nonviolent people? Nothing of this as yet. We are spectators, bystanders, or perhaps even protagonists, in the Kingdom of Necessity. As yet unrelieved, unredeemed.

≈

A sense of two eras is of the essence here. It will bear repeating: two periods of time are involved, not one. The first is the era of actual event: the era of the victimized and vindicated; of those enslaved, then set free. And the era as well of the necessary foil, the victimizers, woefully punished. The second era is the Solomonic, the time of plenary triumph. In that era, the account under our eyes is set down, long after are the events recounted. The former victims, alas, have adopted the ways of their neighbors. Under David and Solomon, an imperial entity has taken form. Final form in more ways than one. Final, as is stipulated grandly in decrees and prayers and pronunciamentos.

As also has been suggested, powerful Israel has come to resemble the hated Egyptians. Israel now boasts grandiose architecture, imposes forced labor, fosters class divisions, wages wars unending, celebrates its heroes and their exploits (and exploitations).

~

And what of the god? Inevitably, it seems, the deity is assimilated, this time to the "people of choice." The god and his votaries alike prevail and prosper. The priesthood is a fraternity of acolytes, useful to the king's devices, inscribed on the king's payroll, along with other functionaries useful to the court.

And what of prophets? We have Nathan, sporadically outspoken, as often as not morally inconsistent. And Samuel: hardly an improvement. We judge them harshly, jaundiced as we are by knowledge of heroes yet unborn.

~

EXODUS 12

In any case, on to the paschal celebration and its ambiguous overtones. The divine imperative is unmistakably stern: thou shalt, thou shalt not. We hear a tone that will sound again on Mount Sinai.

The sense of detail in Exodus 12 is also notable: A specified time and place, a specific menu and stance while eating; all these converge in a rite that will remain essentially unchanged for millennia. The ritual is a feat of energetic communal memory. The vast freight of saving events is borne along in a splendid caravan of images, across a terrain of time hardly less daunting than the Judean desert. Pogroms, crusades, Holocaust, the state of Israel, the redoubtable Palestinians, a terrifying tit for tat, the second intifada. The span reaches from around 1310 CE to our nascent millennium.

And beyond doubt the procession will wend its way over the horizon of the next century and on and on, while time lasts.

~

That pascal lamb, always dying, never dies. We Christians have seized on the image for our own rite of passage. (And what of the implications of the rite—what of the nonviolence of the Victim slain? Alas, small comprehension or change of heart. Instead, yet another American war, the church silent, or proffering yet another "just war" justification).

The key word governing the Christian passover, it seems, is *innocence*. An innocence that creates a like virtue in others, invites simplicity and candor in those who partake of the banquet. An innocence that excludes no one, admits of no enmities, no transfer of guilt. An innocence gently inclusive—even of ourselves, our sins. An innocence honored by the guilty as well.

Right understanding, above all, and an open circle of celebrants! To our feast in the third millennium Egyptian children, too, are invited along with Hebrew children, American (black, brown, yellow, white) children, Iraqi children, and Cuban children, and Afghan children. Parents, loins girt, stand beside the children. All are welcome—and not only to a symbolic cut of lamb.

A truth most solemn is celebrated and embraced here; all are to undertake the same exodus. All have been enslaved; all have need of an intercessor, of a suffering Servant who will halt the scapegoating of the old gods and their devotees, the oppressors.

This is the radical Christian midrash on the ancient rite: Christ is the Lamb, in life and death, in crime and consequence. The old game stops here, that immemorial transfer of the burden of crime from criminal to victim. No more of that. The preeminent Victim declares, the game has been played out once for all in My flesh.

~

This is the new Game, risen from the dust and ashes and dry bones of the old. Only the innocent save; only those (that One) who submitted to death—and who, in that awesome choice, have refused to inflict death. The One and the multitude, the type and antitype, the Martyr and the martyrs—they are slain; and they save.

They save us as well, from the "second death," from the will, pernicious and perennial, to inflict death.

Thus the hymn:

> To the paschal Lamb
> slain,

We Christians
offer praise . . .

The Lamb
has saved the flock.

Thanks
to Jesus innocent,

sinners
are reconciled.

Life and Death,
locked
in stupendous struggle—

The King of Life
dies—

No!

He lives,
He reigns!

~

The book of Revelation invites us to ponder the vast scope of implication; the image of Christ under the rubric of "the Lamb who was slain" (Rev 5:6).

> The seer weeps bitterly,
> "for no one is found worthy to open . . . the scroll."
> He is comforted by an elder:
> "Do not weep . . . The Lion . . . has won by His victory the right to
>   open the scroll . . ."
> The seer turns, and sees
> "a Lamb standing . . ." (Rev 5:4–6)

Lion and Lamb. A double image, tension and irony, majesty and meekness, one prevailing and submitting. A conjunction of opposites: Victim and Victor.

≈

Let us pause to ponder, as well, the vocation of those ancient Egyptian children and their counterparts: the victims of our own day, Iraqi children dying under American sanctions. Can it be that those children, lambs sacrificed for the sins of their pharaoh (and the sins of our pharaohs) will save us, even us?

≈

Paul, writing (as has been speculated) in the springtime, in the paschal season, reminds the community of Corinth that

> Christ,
> our pasch
> (-al Lamb),
>
> has
> been
> immolated.

The believers are to celebrate the death and resurrection of the Lamb, not with the "old leaven of malice and perversity," but with the *azymes*,

> the
> unleavened
> bread
>
> of sincerity
> and
> truth. (1 Cor 5:7–8)

≈

The "immolation" of the ancient Egyptian children was an act of unspeakable divine-human violence. Time passes, and the decree yields a different outcome. On the part of Jesus, sacrificial murder is transformed—better, transfigured. His life is surrendered, a gift—the gift of life itself. Thus the former miasmic behavior is done with, once for all.

And in the act of Jesus's giving His life, God's secret is out: Who God is.

Here in rather fumbling prose, a sound point is made;

> The phrase "God is love" (1 John 4:8) . . . is the end result of a process of human discovery which constitutes a slow and complete subversion from within, of any other perception of God.
>
> That God is love is a certainty achieved in the degree to which it came to be discovered that God has nothing to do with human violence and death; and as it became clear that God has so little to do with those things that he was capable of subverting them through Jesus' being expelled as a sinner, to show that the goodness and justice of God have nothing to do with our fatal and expulsive *[sic]* notions of goodness and justice.
>
> The perception that God is love has a specific content which is absolutely incompatible with any perception of God as involved in violence, separation, anger or exclusion.[18]

—James Alison, English theologian

~

The murder of the children proceeds apace, at the behest of the god. We underscore this, one of the most terrible verses of the Bible:

> At midnight the Lord smote all the firstborn in the land of Egypt, from the firstborn of Pharaoh to the firstborn of the captive in the dungeon . . . (Exod 12:29)

~

Still, one day a light will shine, defeating the blear of this night. The words "At midnight, the Lord" (Exod 12:29) will be summoned as an indictment of the god, as a witness for the prosecution. The one who does such things is the deity of a criminal people—ourselves.

Thus the Bible subverts the Bible. And for Christians, the ultimate Subverter is God in Christ Jesus.

～

"Without vision, the people perish." The ancient proverb captures the personal and political truth of our difficult time. Our society groans under the weight of blindness, denial, woundedness, violence, injustice and alienation. This is no more apparent than in the present moment, as we struggle to come to terms with the meaning of September 11, '01. In such times it is incumbent on people of faith to offer a history so enslaved to "an eye for an eye" that we have all become blind.

Regaining vision is both a gift and a task. It means first looking again to our wisdom traditions and sacred stories, because they are older and wiser than we, and can tell us where we've gone wrong. This in turn leads us to revise our view of how things are, questioning dominant social orthodoxies and embracing those who are marginalized by them. And this animates a revisioning of what could be in our lives and in the world. Only such a process can break our spell of passivity and credulity, ignite our imaginations and empower us . . . in personal healing and social change.

—*Ched Myers, American activist and theologian*

～

Verse 37 and following

The Hebrews depart, great numbers of them, a multitude, some six hundred thousand men, it is said, "without counting their families" (Exod 12:37).

But . . . but . . . Our script is a narrative of imperial hyperbole. Let the skies be the limit! Vast numbers are summoned, and hints, too, are laid on the page, of the beginnings of great wealth.

Wonderful are the ironies history brings to term. The Solomonic mind thus reasons: it is greatly to our advantage to show how adroitly we've imitated the Egyptians—indeed, have bested them on their own ground. Take note of us then, a vast people grown conscious of aborning power and of material wealth rightfully accruing—even in slavery! By double or triple right, or more, as compensation for four and a half centuries of slavery!

So. The booty falls to them like a Danaean rain of gold. And it serves the designs of later arrivistes to linger over the sources and to sacralize them. It is by will of Yahweh no less (always the deity is invoked in shady matters) that the departing tribe, lately freed under the same exalted auspices, precipitously falls on the wealth of their persecutors.

Let the silver and gold and jewels and rich vestments be thought of as a (not-so-occult) payment come due. Amen and alleluia and vast satisfaction, a triple nimbus embracing the plunder. And more, and better: Yahweh wills it!

~

EXODUS 13

This puzzling god strides ahead of Moses, talking of new prescriptions. Poor Moses can hardly keep abreast.

The movements of this god are puzzling to us as well, if not on occasion inducing a stronger reaction: a rising of the gorge. For instance; a claim is laid on the first-born male, whether human or beast: each is to be consecrated to Yahweh.

Verses 8 and 14

The memory of the choice must be kept close and renewed annually. When questioned by a son as to the meaning of the rite, the father is to respond:

> With a strong hand
> the Lord

> brought us
> out of Egypt,

> that place
> of slavery.

> When pharaoh
> stubbornly refused
> to let us go,

the Lord
killed
every
firstborn

in
the land

of
Egypt . . .

Linger over the event with a kind of lupine satiation:

first-
born
of
man

and
of
beast. (Exod 13:14–15)

~

We have a story of winners and losers and the turning of tables. The imperial slaveholders lose out, in ways terrible to tell. And the slaves? They and their children emerge safe. And the supreme accolade is theirs: the favor of the divinity, an unfading, verdant crown, age on age.

More and yet more: great works accompany the choice and the passing of the laurel from one generation to another.

~

Still it must be insisted; we have here a bad game, whether the contestants be celestial or earthly, or whether, among themselves, humans square off in war. A bad game: winners and losers. A fiction as well, a cruel one, self-deceiving, self-defeating.

Its true name: losers and losers each and all. No winners. And more: a not-so-subtle mimesis is at work amid the killing, as becomes clear afterward. (Or does not!)

Granted, the former winners are the present losers, and vice versa. But as smoke and mirrors yield to the light of day (the light of true memory and conscience restored), a truth emerges: The new winners closely resemble the former, whom they have defeated and humiliated.

The like game, awful.

A bad game for all who play. Name them. Bad for the god who devises the rules and nudges the game on and on as good, as virtuous, as his bounden will.

And on earth as in heaven: bad. Which is to say demeaning, brutalizing, cynical, morally abysmal, boneheaded, futile, for Hebrews and Egyptians alike. Both parties ethically degraded, each complicit in works and pomps of death.

(Read: in this mad spring of 2002, the same for Americans and bin Ladenites. And the children of Afghanistan and Iraq paying dearly).

~

The god has brought a halt to centuries of slavery but what of means and ends? Contriving a fortunate outcome, he has out-pharaohed the pharaoh.

Here is the unsweet outcome: there will be other slaves, other slave masters. The god has presided at a change of decor, of costume, of status. But hearts (including his heart) have hardened. "The more things change, the more they remain the same."

~

How much the god must learn, how much renounce and unlearn!

And soon or late (perhaps too late) he must take note (and perhaps regret) the hazardous direction in which even now he is moving the "chosen."

A cloud stands on the horizon. Presently it is no larger than a human hand. In time, it will consume the sun. A presumption, foolish and ruinous, both; in the face of crises to come, the god and the covenanted will launch an extermination policy.

Once a given crisis is resolved, presumably the policy will be abandoned; all said, it was a last-ditch expedient, a once-and-only.

How crookedly reasoned! Should not a god know better? The first "expedient" will shortly give rise to another and then to another. There will be no end of "just causes," crises not of our making, each demanding huge bloodlettings.

No end from the time of the conquest of Canaan and on to this, our dark millennium.

~

Almost at hand is the first crisis facing the parties to the exodus. To wit: this promised land "flowing with milk and honey" has been occupied from ancient times. Indeed, the god is precise, ticking off names of occupants one by one, these doomed unchosen.

Meantime, a shift of scene.

Can the Canaanite tribes be imagined as standing idle, neglecting the plow or the planting of vineyards or the harvest to welcome openhandedly a band of arrivistes set on evicting them? Folly.

A rich catalogue of peoples flourishes beyond the Jordan. They stand proud in possession and achievement:

"Canaanites, Hittites, Amorites, Hivvites, Jebusites" (Exod 13:5).

It is through their labors and skills that the land 'flows with milk and honey.

~

Here is the decree: Be they damned. Vast numbers of these inhabiting tribes are marked (the traditions differ, but each is dire) for eviction, assimilation, or death. Their offense is quite simple: they stand in the way.

~

Does the episode bear a distressingly familiar look? Must we not speak of the plight of the Palestinian people today, as their Israeli masters seize land and chattels, imprison without trial, demolish homes, reduce a people to generational serfdom?

A familiar look, recalling the history of the blacks of South Africa under apartheid? Or the fate of indigenous peoples of Guatemala or Brazil or the United States?

Or in the mad autumn of 2001, a familiar look. An obscure hand-ful of men attack the impregnable U.S. of A. and die even as they kill. The vast towers fall to rubble. The wanton act launches a massive assault against Afghanistan and Iraq. And the old story is told once more: on both sides, many innocents perish.

~

Where, one asks, where is to be found the story of these charged events of the exodus told by Egyptians? What of their memories? What might an Egyptian father tell a child who survived the exterminating angel, a second or third child of the night of blood? And a harder question by far: what memory would the Egyptians pass on, concerning the Hebrews and the god of the Hebrews? Execration? Hatred? Vows of reprisal?

~

By will of a rival deity, Egypt, the oppressor, has been mightily oppressed by plagues, culminating in a draconian decree against the firstborn. And Yahweh has decreed against them even worse, a kind of ultimate larceny. Egypt is denied a story.

It would seem important that we refuse to act as mindless parti-sans of the god of Israel. We refuse to conclude Egypt has no story worth telling.

(As a famous prime minister of modern Israel was wont to ask with more than a tinge of contempt, "But these 'Palestinians,' who are they?")

~

We have dwelt long on the "game" of Yahweh and on the players. And being privy to the outcome, we are in position (I dare say endowed with the vocation) to judge. In a modest sense to hold the god accountable, to-gether with his works. And to hold the players accountable—the chosen as well as the rejected.

~

Is a properly biblical game being played out here, played out in subtle ways, in ways often lost sight of? Is this a slanted history? Biased? (And, furthermore, is the game aided and abetted by commentators lugging along their baggage of parti pris?)

Skilled in the game is our scribe, a master of inference and irony. His story is like a drama by Shakespeare or Pirandello, a game within the game. A subtle, seemingly improvisational theme shadows the grand main one.

It is as though before an audience a clown were speaking, sotto voce, an unwelcome truth. Or as though a court fool, finger to his lips, were holding the large theme aloft in a mocking cartoon.

Thus a clue as to the method of our storyteller. He is at heart an impassioned judge, a fervent ethician. Events, motives, movements of the spirit (whether the protagonists sit on heavenly or earthly thrones, no matter): these are closely recorded, weighed, found acceptable or wanting.

He would have us, in our place of advantage (a later testament in our hands, and its prodigious finalities), drawn into the drama, playing the omniscient observers, the wise ancients. Or, not to forget, playing the court fools in the court of heaven or earth or both. The foolishness conceals a deeper wisdom than that of the pharaoh, for that matter deeper than the wisdom of Moses.

Deeper than even Yahweh can summon?

In any case, the text is to be thought inspired in more senses than one. We are well advised not to take at face value the behavior of anyone, divine or human, who walks the pages.

The god invites (even as he repels) closest scrutiny of all. We mark his behavior; we take note of his favorite mode, a sometimes-distempered imperative: *Thou shalt; thou shall not!* Certain matters are presented as sacred, inviolate, binding conscience and conduct.

What to make of such matters so presented? The night of exodus is a thick darkness, crowded with spirits ambiguous or evil, with whisperers, berserkers even. It would engulf us, too.

～

In sum, the text demands literate readers. They ponder closely; when required, they go counter to the text. With this understanding: to object, even to reject, is to come closer to the original intent, that the Bible may prove of service to ethical maturity in the world.

To put the matter closely, not any god will do. Not necessarily or finally or convincingly, the god of the book of Exodus.

Dare it; true God must prove godly, or we languish among idols.

~

The text is to be weighed in light of experience, in light of other later texts, in accordance with the analogy of faith. Thus, the Exodus story waits on us for translation, for enactment, for critique, for admiration.

For rejection and judgment as well—a parlous undertaking and crucial. Does the text wait on our anger, our indignation? How could it not be so?

~

Claims, rules, choices, liturgies of rejoicing in a freedom wrestled from the depths—these require counterclaims, broken rules, liturgies of repentance. Repentance for the death of children, whether Egyptian or Hebrew (or Iraqi or Cuban or South African or Northern Irish or Afghan), repentance for these lambs sacrificed to whose advantage, to whose edification?

Thus, the paschal rite as mandated falls under scrutiny. This, though the text presents it baldly, as tribal, exclusionary, celebrating by implication the murder of the innocent.

~

And the question is never done with: the god, what of him? On a day far distant from the present text, this deity will be sternly instructed, even resisted verbally and symbolically by the great prophets. They will denounce (former) favorites, defend the vulnerable, the "widow and orphan and stranger at the gate." They will question the tactics of kings, disobey bad laws conscientiously, denounce royal wars, demand truthful worship, shake and dismantle realms of power and might.

~

A double time frame, as has been suggested, is a clue to the character of the deity of Exodus. This version of the god bears the heavy accoutrements of the deity resident in Solomon's temple.

Centuries pass; events are recorded in our text—momentous events: the arrival and occupation of Canaan, the rise and decline of the judges, the onset of monarchy, and the rise of the empire under David and Solomon.

The god of the desert and the god of the Jerusalem temple: these are conflated during the monarchy as one and the same: in thunderations of "obey or else," in jealousies, in a tendency to strike down and raise up unpredictably, in a plenum of cruelties and sacralized wars, in lightning bolts launched even against true believers.

We recall the attempted murder of Moses (Exod 4:24–26) and, centuries later, the death of Uzzah, luckless bearer of the ark, along the road to Jerusalem (2 Sam 6:6–7). This god is untamed, unpredictable, unmollified by female sensibility. He is like a great male lion, apt on a whim to strike out and kill even the cubs he has sired.

And inevitably, the image suggests an opposite: the prophets. On a rare occasion when one or another "lioness" of a prophet is allowed entrance, she stands vigil on behalf of the helpless and victimized.

~

Onward and upward this people rises from a ragtag tribe of nomads to mastery in the world. And along with them comes the "developed" god of the imperium. That one, it must be concluded, differs in no important aspect of attitude and behavior from the god of Exodus. Of old, he decreed the slaughter of children. Later, he stands firm beside warriors and chiefs, with David and Solomon, the darlings of a grand design of empery, his realm and theirs tight as warriors' handclasps.

~

And the original wars (those "necessary," "just" wars endemic to the conquest of Canaan), they went on and on. Inevitably, new necessities arose—and how could it not be so, "in the nature of things"? In the nature of war itself, or of empire: those awesome interchangeable mutualities, the one being the health of the other.

~

The law of Exodus, the law of empire: time will reveal them as one and the same. First, in view of the seizure of Canaan, such wars were "necessary for survival," subject to a law of "expand or perish." Then there developed a favored way of life among the elite of Jerusalem. Such would hardly favor second thoughts concerning conflict and bloodletting. And the god would seem to agree. No second thoughts from on high.

It was equally clear that the forced laborers, the hoplites of the standing armies, the slaves and indentured—these would be granted no voice, no access or relief.

The domestic victims, the expendables, are in place; they are born there, live there, die there. How else put it? The chosen have created a domestic egyptical-style social pyramid, an unalterable economic, military, religious system. Time now is imperial time; it has the force of a dogma; what is shall be, forever and ever.

No relief, not yet. Not until Isaiah and his word of a deity, of a God (dare we say?) "reborn."

How long humans must wait for the good news, long as the generational sighing of slaves born, slaves slaving, slaves dying. So long that the powerful, secure in their status, ceased even to fear or imagine the unthinkable. Word, that is, of a God Who speaks contrarily. Then at long last: "'My ways are not your ways,' said the Lord" (Isa 55:9).

Who longed for such a word? Who hoped for it in the night of the long swords? Who dared utter the word? We know their names; they are the oracles of the new God, the midwives of the new creation.

The kings who sat the throne in Jerusalem, along with their underlings, heard the word with dread. The response was quick; punishment, often condign, met the likes of Isaiah, Jeremiah, Ezekiel.

~

Verse 17 and following

So begins the grand march. It has become a master symbol of every going-forth of every age: the quest for a god, for a home, for one's own soul, for one another.

~

"Spiritual path" is the hilarious popular term for those night-blind mesas and flayed hills in which people grope, for decades on end, with the goal of knowing the absolute. They discover others spread under the stars and encamped here and there by watch fires, in groups or alone, in the open landscape; they stop for a sleep, or for several years, and move along without knowing toward what or why. They leave whatever they find, picking up each stone, carrying it awhile, and dropping it gratefully and without regret, for it is not the absolute, though they cannot say what is. Their life's fine, impossible goal justifies the term "spiritual."

Nothing however can justify the term "path" for this bewildered and empty stumbling, this blackened vagabondage—except one thing—They don't quit. They stick with it. Year after year they put one foot in front of the other, though they fare nowhere. Year after year they find themselves still feeling with their fingers for lumps in the dark.[19]

—*Annie Dillard, American essayist, poet, and novelist*

~

Verses 17 and 18

At the start of the grand hegira, two themes stand out. One is the complicity in violence:

Armed
cap to toe,

the Israelites
went
out. (Exod 13:18)

And Yahweh leads the people the long way round the Philistine territory. Since, he reasons,

should
the people
see
that they

must
do battle,

they

might change

their resolve

and return

to

Egypt. (Exod 13:17)

Then, what relief, a striking contrast!

For the second theme, one almost forgave violent Yahweh and his armed tribe. We have a sudden change in the ethical climate, radiant images of protection and guidance. Day and night, a presence hovers near; a pillar of cloud or a pillar of fire precedes the caravan.

The images are alive, and grow. Eventually, the *shekinah* of glory will hover above the temple. In other texts, the pillar of fire is evoked as a mysterious movement of "devouring flame," an image of Yahweh. And perennially dear to the mystics of later ages is the "cloud of unknowing."

~

EXODUS 14

Verse 21 and following

A theme of grandeur and a further deliverance. The first was through land. Now, equally spectacular, through water—the passage through the Red Sea.

Of the wonders worked there, what has not been recited, sung, mimed, danced, painted, sculpted—a hundred times, a thousand—in tones and colors and costumes and sounds bespeaking awe and admiration? The trumpets, the conquest of nature through the god of nature, the prevailing—the sense in sum (surely Solomonic!) of a people who ride high and mighty in the saddle of history.

Hearken now, all nations; through "Yahweh, the warrior," the underdog has emerged triumphant! And only look about you; god and ruler are ensconced in befitting grandeur—the temple and palace of the imperial city. How splendidly we—and our god—have prevailed!

~

EXODUS 15

Verses 1–17

Irony upon irony is heaped, the empire in full bloom. And the Jerusalemites compose a chant of victory in derision of another empire, the Egyptian.

Let the irony be noted; it is scalding. Those who compose the chant and sing it aloud: "We, the conquerors, in our violence, in our engines and enterprises, in our political and military (and yes, religious) styles and rubrics—how nearly we come (how nearly we have come!) to resemble the hated oppressor of old.

This is the implication of the chant. Against monstrous odds, there arose a kingdom like no other, past or imagined. A virtuous empire, a holy people, a holy city, the co-creation of the god and his chosen.

The glance of the scribe falls to the page; he marvels and writes. The miracle is beyond critique or marring. No speck in this perfect eye!

~

This is the outcome, as time eventually reveals, time that cuts to the bone every artifice of clothing and flesh, until the skeleton stands free to rattle its tale, at long last truthfully.

No speck, perfect eye? Only wait; a very plank will come in view—and will be plucked therefrom. Witness those troublesome spirits biding their moment in the wings of time nearing: Isaiah, Jeremiah, and the others. And the embarrassing matters they will persist in raising. (And this, we note, in the era that produced the triumphant song of Moses and Miriam.) Matters like enslavement and forced labor, inordinate wealth and misery, contempt for the victims, sanctioned violence, wars and incursions.

And who, they thunderously inquire, dares claim that Yahweh approves all this? The prophets indignantly deny it, the calumny. Thus instructing over their shoulder, as it were, Yahweh the omnipresent. "What of the appalling injustice in our midst?" they will cry. And Yahweh will grow thoughtful.

~

These lucid spirits enter history, and it is as though a school of Socrates has flowered in Jerusalem. Such questions they pose, such contradiction

of inhuman ways, of riches questionably accruing, of larcenies and betrayals, of religious rites that like perfume in a charnel house, sweeten the
stench of death.

"What," they shout. "What of that phenomenon named 'worship'?
What god would take pleasure in the witless incantations of a criminal
people? Would such a god differ in any respect from a baal? Are not the
spectacles of the sanctuary to be accounted inconsequential, infected as
they are with the greed of priests and the violence of public life?"

Voices of rectitude and consequence will lie about, like a scourge.
And the god will grow thoughtful, aroused.

Then, along with his vocalists, he will grow indignant. And according to Ezekiel, an utterly astounding event ensues. The deity abandons
the temple, departs in exile, stigmatizing the place as a befouled nest of
idolatry (Ezek 10:18–19).

~

The above reflections perhaps anticipate or wander far. And perhaps not.
Call them simply an attempt to offer a sense of the atmosphere in which
the famous "Victory Chant" arose.

The miraculous parting of the waters was long past, but the memory
persisted, elaborating the wonders that preceded arrival in Canaan. Not,
surely, "arrival" in the sense of mere survival, the sorry tale of a tribe long
beset, crossing over into the unknown.

Nothing of this. By worldly standards (are other standards respect-
ed here?), another far greater achievement is celebrated. Conquest of
Canaan was one matter, and due thanks for it. Another triumph awaited;
the secular apogee: equality among the nations. And more than equality. Surpassing all others—the chosen, their god, and the darling of the
apogee, Solomon.

A mere tribe among tribes has become a peerless warrior people,
an imperium. And their deity? He *[sic]* dwells in a splendid temple. His
approval is bestowed on all sides and comers (well, nearly all!), a veritable
rain of gold!

Mutual subversion and stroking, dovetailing of the transcendent
and worldly. These, together with ever-widening boundaries of moral allowance. The king can do no wrong!

Neither, of course, can the deity. The decalogue, a stern enough code, is inscribed in stone on a temple wall. And for the most part is honored in the breach, in lip service.

Behold, the sensibility that evoked the song. Hardly Mosaic in spirit, Solomonic rather:

> Praise Yahweh,
> praise to the skies!
>
> Horse and chariot
> plunged in the sea!
>
> Yahweh my strength,
> theme of my song,
> my deliverer, my god.
>
> No more
> the chariots of the pharaoh,
>
> no more
> the walking forest of doom.
>
>   Down, down the throat
> of a voracious sea,
> a watery abyss—
>
> down they went,
> a stone in the sea's pocket.
>
> Your right hand
> broke them—
>
> a bundle of sticks.
>
> Your wrath arose;
> they vanished,
> chaff in a firestorm.

Prodigious,
    your breath
blew once only—

the waves rose;
they were no more.

The enemy said
in his heart:

"Pursue them,
o'ertake them,

cut them asunder,
devour them whole!"

No.
    You breathed once, and
the sea
took them for prey.

The lead of a plumb line
measured, found wanting—

    them,
snatched
from the land of the living.

To whom
shall we liken you
artisan,
your prodigious works?

You raised a hand,
the maw of Sheol
closed

whelmed—
warrior,
chariot,
horses.

You,
ever gracious,

launched your people,
        a sped arrow
straight
toward the promise.

You raise right arm,
the nations
petrified stand—

among stone images
baals—

hapless,
helpless
to interpose—

your people
        pass, free.

You led us forth,
you plant us
verdant

upon a holy mountain

    yours, ours,
this sanctum

fashioned
of no human hands. (Exod 15:1–18)

~

One cannot but note; the tone and imagery are hardly of a tribe on the run. Rather, the poetry implies a sophisticated, prosperous political entity quite sure of itself. Sure also of approval from on high. What "magnalia," what deeds worthy of praise!

Is the god also a judge? To be sure, but the god is also subtly judged, weighed in the scales of vaulting pride. Thus the momentous reversal wrought by the Empire. That entity gains a capital letter, even as the god loses one.

Until the prophets.

~

At the start of his public life, Jeremiah issues first a momentous reversal, a great "No":

This day

I
set you

over
nations

and
kingdoms;

to root up
and tear down,

to

destroy

and

to

demolish ...

Then follows the birth of right order, a new start, a laconic resounding
"Yes":

... to

build

and

to

plant. (Jer 1:9)

Exodus 15–20

EXODUS 15

Verse 22 and following

Let the newly freed learn at the start: the way to the promise will be rocky and chancy indeed.

The pilgrims come to a place of bitter waters. And an ominous hint rises on the air. A "murmuring" breaking out at every setback. Then, the unpredictable mood of Yahweh. "What shall we drink?" That hum of discontent! In the transcendent ear, it sounds like a hive of wasps, grievously annoyed—and annoying.

Has the god forsooth not stood by them, named them his own? Was not a series of plagues loosed against their oppressors and a path laid out for themselves? Was not the sea parted for safe passage?

~

Salvation through the waters and, now, what irony! The issue once more is—water. Ungrateful, capricious, buzzing clan! Such misconduct merits a sharp warning. Let them take note; the divine favor is strictly conditional.

And we have the first of a historical barrage of *ifs*. The monosyllable will sound a constant beat through the desert years and on to the era of kings. Again and again a strictly conditional favor is sounded, an *if* from on high: to Moses, later to Saul (in vain), to David (who wavers between fealty and crime), to Solomon (that luxurious reprobate).

Prophets too will drum the ancient theme. This: the favor of Yahweh is strictly conditioned on behavior measured against the law. The great "if" is laid against obeisance to "ordinances . . . observances . . . commandments . . . laws."

~

The God of Jesus, be it noted with gratitude, speaks no such "if." In Him, we are free of a god whose commands are captive to our behavior, good or ill. In Christ, we note a pure gratuity, no tags. Divine love is vivacious, unconditioned.

~

A new understanding is laid out plain:

> God
> so loved
> the world
>
> as to give
>
> God's
> only
> Son . . . (John 3:16)

And yet another word of Jesus, uttered the night before His death, a word of sublime access to the heart of God:

> having loved
> his own . . .
>
> loved
> them
>
> to
> the
> end. (John 13:1)

What that "end" was would stand on the morrow, stark and cruciform for all to see. And what fury "the world" (which is to say ourselves) wreaked against the Gift of the Father is also plain. To our remorse—and our hope as well. In Him.

But such events and the insights they offer lie far in the future. In the exodus, we are after all in the era of the law. Terrible to say, the god is captive to "commands and statutes." He reigns over a Kingdom of Necessity, raises scales on high, closely weighs merit and demerit, responds accordingly. Judgment darkens the air. Divine-human intercourse, if it is to prosper, is undertaken as a strict quid pro quo.

~

Terrible is the analogy drawn by Yahweh or at least implied. Is this "murmuring," this undercurrent of unrest and revolt, is this to be thought superior to the behavior of the Egyptians, faithless as these were presumed to be? Let the chosen mend their ways. The plagues that brought Egypt to its knees lurk also, a cloud charged with lightnings, above themselves.

~

Happily, the episode closes on a different note, a kind of edenic diminuendo. Before the caravan enters the harsh, brooding desert, a pause for encampment. And relief is at hand.

Someone, our author, is gifted with a vivid memory. He summons blessings that hover like a perfume on the temperate air. Harmonious nature! With open arms a pleasant oasis greets the caravan.

The place is called Elim; it is graced with—only imagine, after the bitter waters and the equally bitter warning—pure poetry; this:

> twelve
> springs
> of water
>
> and
> seventy
> palm trees. (Exod 15:27)

Awhile they settle there and take their ease, this flock of lorn peregrines. Then they break camp. Onward, into the desert places and a series of acute testings.

The episode of the manna opens, beyond doubt a parable hearkening back to the 'days of creation' and the benign Creator.

(And one thinks, with a measure of bitterness, of great chances missed, neglected, even despised throughout history. A parable for today as well).

~

EXODUS 16

We note the close union, wrought in vast dramatic scale, of creation and salvation. The deity who contrives the providential food and rains it down, forty years of day-to-day sustenance, is revealed in the prodigious act, as savior of the people. Is revealed (were we humans not blind as bats at midday) as the openhearted, open-handed dispenser of the good things of creation.

The poorest of the poor are the beneficiaries, a make-do people of tents, poles, and nondescript bundles, a caravan of nomads. They lack all recourse save one; they are close kept under the wing of providence.

~

Eden, in a desert? Is this a reversal, temporary, heartbreakingly fragile, of the Fall itself? It would seem so. A storm of sweet nourishment, a windfall of bounty; unfailing, the manna falls.

And one is led to reflect; a renewed world might look like this. Manna day by day, six days of gifts from the heavens—a trustful spirit, the god coming through, hunger assuaged. Bounty and benefit touching everyone. No one claiming too much or enduring too little; no misery, because no overweening wealth. Heaven come to our world?

Then, on day seven, a break in the beneficent routine. On the day previous, a double portion fell. The sabbath. No need below, no gift from above. In both realms, sweet rest and repose.

~

A further point. Yahweh, giver of manna, is much improved in the giving. This, too, is an element of the parable. Needy humans evoke the bounty of the god.

A changed demeanor! Now the deity wears a mothering look, grows imaginative and compassionate, savior of the needy.

The god remembers, and the god forgets, as it pleases. And we praise, and are wary. This deity is chancy as a tornado, not tamed to the measure of our tropes—like this, unlike that.

No, he resembles and dissembles, both. He moves in darkness, inexplicably. He ignores high crime; and with little or no provocation is apt to strike out with a lethal blow.

Still, for the present, for the time of gift giving, he forgets those other awful initiatives: condemnation, vengeance, incitements to war, olympian thunderations.

~

We Christians have seen another, later time of gift giving. The God who gave the manna has a greater gift in mind; "his only begotten Son." Thus the story of the manna is handed on and on. In due course, it touches the imagination of Christ, is munificently enlarged, a midrash of the Gospel of John (John 6:26–58):

> I
> solemnly
>
> assure
> you,
>
> it was not Moses
> who gave you
>
> bread
> from the heavens;
>
> it is my Father
> who gives you
>
> the real
> heavenly bread.
> God's bread
> comes down
> from heaven

and

gives life

to
the
world. (John 6:47–51)

~

The original event has become transhistorical. The savory flakes that once fell and fell are held in ecstasy before our eyes. With this implication: the ancient gift, wonderful as it was, cannot exhaust the theme. Its meaning awaits penetration by this One, the true Manna.

And the manna as "sign," cannot do full justice to the Event-to-come; the One Signified has walked in our midst, a pure Bestowal.

~

Astonishing, this lengthy discourse recorded by John. We note the changes rung, the lapidary contrasts set up, in timing, in the noble personages summoned:

. . . not Moses
gave . . .

bread
in the desert . . .

and

my Father
gives . . .

real
heavenly
bread. (John 6:32)

The Source of the bread (in more senses than one) is noted; and at length, the Bread is named aright; it is "from heaven." Mind and heart linger enchanted as the past is made present; Moses "gave"; "my Father gives." The God who dwells outside time, within time gives and gives.

This is the mark and meaning of each moment of a lifetime, of a generation, of all generations: the manna that falls and falls, the Gift that offers "life to the world." To ourselves life.

~

Do we credit it, that there is in our God nothing of death?

> As to the fact that the dead are raised, have you not read what God said to you: "I am the God of Abraham, the God of Isaac, the God of Jacob"?

> He is God of the living, not of the dead. (Matt 22:32)

~

Another scribe concurs, in the book of Wisdom. Death enters the world, but hardly through God's doing. No, let responsibility be precise, let the finger of truth point. The human tribe, ourselves. We court death, that veiled skeleton-bride;

> Court not death
> by your erring
> way of life,
>
> nor draw
> to yourselves
> destruction,
>
> by the works
> of your hands.
>
> Because
> God
>
> did not
> make death,

nor does God
rejoice

in
the destruction
of the living.

For God
fashioned all

that
they might
have
being . . . (Wis 1:12–14)

~

In stark contrast, there is in our world a parsimony of life, of love of life, of givers of life. And there is much, overmuch, a tidal wave, an eruption, a dizzy conspiracy and confabulation, of death. A vast panoply, armies, air forces, Trident submarines, cruise missiles, depleted uranium-tipped missiles capable of making rubble of a hundred worlds. A technological plague of the methods and metaphors of death.

Pre-Christian we are in our understanding of God—of the gods, rather: those inscrutable forces that await a summons to nudge our death-ridden appetites.

And post-Christian (posthuman?) we Americans are, in dazzling techniques—making death available, desirable, cheap, indiscriminate, quick, issuing like a gorgon from sky and sea and land.

Death, the omnivorous, the cannibal. The close crony of socialized despair.

~

Thus, the law of death, verified yet once more in the aftermath of September, 2001. All else failing (closer the truth: nothing else tried)— America launches a barrage of bombs, destroys humans; perturbs, perhaps irreparably, the sweet creation.

The new millennium is a permanent cold war, frozen in place and time, a permafrost of the heart, an assault against civility, against traditions of the human. In horrid sum, against creation and its God.

~

Exodus chapter 16 is given over to the story of the manna, thirty-six verses. This length suggests that the episode stood central to the scribe—and to the people as well.

Chapter 6 of John's Gospel offers a startling parallel, in the long discourse on the Bread of Life: thirty-three verses.

One is tempted to explore the analogies, the sparks struck. How were the images transformed, and finally, as the Christian midrash suggests, elaborated, elevated? Let us try:

- Both passages are rife with a mood of discontent. Anciently the tribes "murmur" against Moses (Exod 16:2–3). And in face of the words of Christ, many also "murmur" (John 6:41; 6:52; 6:60).

- The exodus folk are exasperated at loss of the "fleshpots of Egypt" (Exod 16:3). And the "crowd" surrounding Jesus is dismayed and angered at his claim:

  "I

  am
  the bread

  that came
  down

  from
  heaven."

  They kept saying,

  "Is this not Jesus,
  the son of Joseph?

Do we not know
his father and mother?

How can he claim
to have come

down
from
heaven?" (John 6:41–42)

~

In face of the complaints in the desert, Yahweh says to Moses;

I am going
to rain bread
from heaven . . .

Thus
I will put them
to the test,

to see
whether
they follow

my
instructions

or
not. (Exod 16:4)

And Jesus to the crowd, in similar terms, demands faith. And thereby
provokes a crisis of faith:

Let me
firmly assure you;

the one
who believes
has
eternal life.

I
am the bread
of life.

Your ancestors
ate manna
in the desert,

but
they died.

This
is the bread

that comes
down from heaven,

for one
to eat

and
never
die. (John 6:47–50)

The "test" is proposed on both occasions. It breaks in pieces a shaky trust. Will they (we) believe, though we have not seen, believe a God who stands by the Word? Believe that the promise, despite our murmuring, our spiritual density—and those years and years of trudging along, of making do, eking out life in the wilderness of a culture of death—despite all, will we believe that the promise holds firm?

~

One is summoned to believe and to follow through on the belief. In the original story, instructions are quite detailed; the later commendations echo them.

Thus, one gathers only enough "manna" for a given day. And on the day preceding sabbath, a double portion is promised; for on the day of rest, no manna falls.

Thus too for the Eucharist. Enough for the day. Tomorrow's needs and hungers will be met. I, Jesus, promise. Believe; there will be bread and bread, for years; from the first communion to the viaticum.

Pray then
in this way:

"Our Father,
who are
in heaven . . .

give us
this day

our
daily
bread . . . (Matt 6:9–11)

~

And in the discourse of Jesus, we note a transition: abrupt, without warning; the "bread" is also "flesh" (with the hint of "fleshpots"?). Mistake it not. He would not have it mistaken; the "bread," rightly taken, is "flesh"—

My
flesh,

for
the life

of

the

world. (John 6:51)

—that phrase, "life of the world," stands in shadow, a haunt in the mind. Knowing, as we do, so much of death, of death overweening in our world. And so little of "life."

Our world—for (small?) good and (vast?) ill. A world that knows little or nothing of life, of the fostering and cherishing of life. A world that knows so much of death.

To such a world is the promise made. To the world we walk, to the world Jesus walked, to the tripped and fallen world.

Say it clear: Jesus is nothing if not clear. Provocative even. Our vocation, which is to say, the human vocation, stands firm, beckons. Despite all. We are to know—life. To learn of life, that the world (that we ourselves) may unlearn death. To learn in a carnal, appetitive way—tasting, eating the manna of life.

~

How much of death in our world, how little of life. How death wins out; how life is snuffed; how the giving of life is a lost art.

~

Former Governor Bush of Texas staked his political career on death and money. The two fonts of political power, rightly understood, are hyphenated: death-money. Bush conducted a juridical death camp in Texas, boasting a staggering array of executions: of women and men, of the retarded, of the guilty and the innocent, of the poor, of people of color. The scythe of the governor cut and cut, indiscriminate and savagely wide.

And his campaigns for the presidency became a continental money grab. He bought, sold, huckstered himself with, expensive, inexorable images of benignity and stalwart firmness: images signifying—nothing, a moral void. The money poured in, an avalanche of oil.

His opponent much resembled him: money, oil, the void.

And are we to forget how the former incumbent firmed up a similar image of executioner and moneyman? As a candidate, Clinton returned to Little Rock to sign the death warrant of a seriously retarded man. And

his wheeling and dealing in office was notorious (and widely admired
and emulated): death-money, the game.

~

In this season of our discontent, the vile game of death-money bursts
beyond national borders, a flood tide over a dam. An international man-
hunt is on for shadowy demonized figures: bin Laden, Hussein. For those
incanted, will-o'-the-wisp "weapons of mass destruction."

~

The "manna" discourse of Jesus marks a turning point for disciples and
for Himself. A crisis: faith stands or falls on adherence to the promise, on
the words of One who, in "the flesh," is long departed from our midst.

   Still, a kind of seizure of the original event has occurred—the new
promise, the astounding premise, stands. The tone is austere; it brooks no
"murmuring." The implication is, take it or leave:

> I
> myself
> am
>
> the living bread
> come down
> from heaven . . .
>
> The bread
> I will give
>
> is
> my flesh,
>
> for
> the life
>
> of
> the
> world. (John 6:51)

And what follows on this unequivocal claim? Division, bitter and unrelieved.

The point is stubborn, underscored, insistent.

Some, those designated "disciples" walk away. Too much.

They are now former disciples.

~

The bread that is "flesh," the "flesh" eaten like bread, daily bread. What could be simpler, or more devastatingly profound—or, rightly understood, more exigent of a last-ditch faith?

We strike up against the words; they strike hard against our notions of "the way things are." They are scandalous to logical minds.

So be it, is the tone; we, too, may take it or leave. Which is to say, "take Me—or leave. I stand by my word, my bread, my flesh."

And what is closer to the person, the person of God, of Jesus, than the word of God, the flesh of God?

~

That "one who believes." The faith of such a one is like the windhover noted by the poet, who saw and marveled at "brute beauty and valor and act."[20] Such faith is the opposite, even the opponent, of the "temperate believer" for whom the "normal" is the only norm—those who "walked no more with Him."

This one, the "one who believes," listens, trusts. Perhaps his prayer is a sorry one; but it is dredged from ardor of soul; "I believe, help my unbelief" (Mark 9:24). Such a one already "has life eternal"—the present mode.

And more:

I
will raise

that
one

on
the

last

day. (John 6:54)

Life eternal, here and now. It penetrates time and culture and household and profession and church assembly, marriage and priesthood, loss and sorrow and joy: all the interstices of life.

Sin also? Sin as well; here, grace prevails, an exorcism, a healing. (It had better, or frozen we are in the cold eye of Jansenists).

And death? Perforce, this life penetrates death, removes its sting, rendering it null and void.

Eternal life, the pledge and promise, in and through temporal life. And the opponent, the conqueror, of sin and death.

What is eternal claims the last word, snatches that word from the shadow whose name is death. Life claims the last word.

And urgent life, like a mouth-to-mouth resuscitation, revives and resurrects the newly dead. The living One confers life. Jesus, say it again:

I

shall raise

that one

on

the

last

day. (John 6:54)

~

Faith does not permit us to fool ourselves. We live amid a welter of megadeath. The apparatus is at ready, the smart bombs are launched, even as these notes are set down. In the gunsights are the innocent and expendable across the world. And more, and worse, in prospect:

> On August 7, 2003, US government scientists and pentagon officials gathered behind tight security at a Nebraska air force base. They discussed the development of a modernized arsenal of small, specialized nuclear weapons which critics believe could mark the dawn of a new era in proliferation. . . .

Requests by congress to send observers were rejected, and an oversight committee which included academic nuclear experts was disbanded only a few weeks earlier.

The purpose of the meeting at Offutt air force base only became known after a draft agenda was leaked earlier this year. It included discussions on a new generation of low-yield 'mini-nukes,' 'bunker-buster bombs' for possible use against rogue states or organizations armed with nuclear, biological or chemical weapons . . .

The place and time of the Offutt meeting is infused with apparently unintended historical irony. The visitors arrived on the anniversary of the Hiroshima bombing and departed on Saturday, the anniversary of the attack on Nagasaki. The B-29 planes which dropped the nuclear bombs, Enola Gay and Bock's Car, were both built at Offutt . . . [21]

—Guardian, *August 7, 2003*

∿

The evidence to the prevailing of "life"—this is thin indeed and fragile, subject in a thousand places to the brutal gunning down of hope. The worldly powers seem hell-bent, literally, bound for hell. Creating in the bleak meantime a hell on earth.

To survive the onslaught of death, we must be nourished, must eat the bread that is flesh. The instruction is quite literal, and shocking: Be carnivores of Christ.

∿

And the awful point of division stands firm. We, too, are free. We may take the word, the word about "my flesh" precisely as it was spoken. The hand is extended; it holds out to us the new manna. Take it, the "bread," the "flesh," it is yours.

Or another course is open—to withdraw, to turn away and to "walk no more with him" (John 6:66).

∿

EXODUS 17

Verses 1–7

Manna falls and falls. The event is immediate, carnal, tender. This for a while; the needs of the body must be met, but the desert cannot meet them. Neither can Moses, unaided. Someone, a greater power, must act. It is a law of survival. So. A crucial intervention is granted. Water has been struck from unyielding barren rock. And now, the life-giving manna.

~

We note and wonder: how consistently bad-spirited these people are! It is as though the daily sweetness from on high turned sour in their guts, did nothing to assuage unfaith, served only to churn up anger. As though in the wayward manner of infants, this daily evidence of benefit—the flakes of food falling gently as snow at dawn, covering the ground with benignity—as though this implied nothing of love, of compassion from on high. The symbol falls and falls. And it falls short.

Each crisis is met as though it were first and only; or worse, as though some prior need had gone unmet. Panic and complaint rend the air. Each time Moses is assailed anew. So is Yahweh, by implication.

Is a deep insight implied? Is this the human predicament, to exist on the instant as though impaled there, to lack sense of continuity, of memory brought to bear, of "this before, and that after" and wisdom accreting?

Little or nothing of this perdurance of memory is indicated in the desert behavior. Something far different, an adolescent immersion in appetite and moodiness, in hungers and thirsts of one sort or another. The people are sunken in the moment—whether of grief or loss or pleasure.

Thus the memory of providence is jettisoned. The misery of the world falls like a hundredweight, is taken as a stolid given, as though God could offer no relief—relief through undimmed hope and open hands.

Granted, desert and wilderness seems apt images of our world and time. But are we to walk moodily, as though we were granted no cooling waters, no manna—no metaphors, no cause to show graciousness toward the Giver?

~

A poet reproves our shabby spirit. He is all but inebriated with "Hurrahing in Harvest":

> And the azurous hung hills are his world-wielding shoulder
>> Majestic—as a stallion stalwart, very-violet-sweet!—
> These things, these things were here and but the beholder
>> Wanting; which two when they once meet,
> The heart rears wings bold and bolder
> And hurls for him, O half hurls earth for him off under
>> his feet.[22]

—*Gerard Manley Hopkins, English poet*

~

Ecstasy. And then something else; what we have made of God's world. Hunger and thirst and refugees and the sad faces of "sanctioned" children, slaughter, starvation, wars unending. To and fro our spirit is tossed.

Then this story meets our eyes. In face of massive improbability, waters are struck from rock, food falls from heaven.

The place where the waters run free is renamed, for remembrance of the event (and hardly an altogether happy memory at that!): *Massa*, "the test" and *Meriba*, "the quarreling."

~

Today, what of today? One does not know, one is not given to know, when or in what form relief will arrive. Children continue to die in great numbers. Presidents and their subalters come and go, validating mechanisms of death, intensifying its lethal scope, pressing on with set purpose, unconcerned.

From the media they meet our horrified gaze, those assured stony faces, women and men alike, power blazing in eyes, abstractions ready on the tongue: "national interest," "collateral damage."

They prosper unchallenged. Let the children die; it is right and just, "we are punishing their leaders," "we consider [the sanctions] worth the price."

~

Verse 8 and following

The tender drama continues; the miraculous waters, the manna.

And then, a shock. We had almost forgotten—our longing for gestures of compassion was so great—perhaps we chose to forget. Then we are brought up short. Yahweh, together with stalwart Moses, is of the warrior breed.

If the chief actors are warriors, their chief image of the world is a battlefield. That being so, let the battle rage. In this episode and those to follow, it will rage on, in the world of Moses or of Jesus (or, to be sure, our own). The god summoned by warriors cannot be other than a warrior god. He blesses the bloodshed. He must.

~

Our scene and era are that of the empire, secured and crowned in Jerusalem. There, a team of scribes reflects on and records the desert years. Battle after battle is told of, and a form of historical parti pris firms up. By war the chosen were certified, justified before the nations, those unappeasable enemies. Israel would survive them, would win their respect (would prosper!), only if, whether in Canaan or the city of David, the chosen were ready and armed, a phalanx of drawn swords.

~

Verses 8–16

Early on, a sequence arose, a matrix and scenario. Preceding each campaign, each battle, Moses undertakes pieties that consecrate the slaughter. Prayer and warfare accord well, for the god, too, is a warrior, pleased with those who in his name unsheathe the sword.

Thus tasks are nicely apportioned between heaven and earth. The role of Moses is prayer, arms outstretched, all the day long. Joshua, who will become famous in a certain way, is to conduct the battle. And Yahweh surveys all from above.

At evening comes a diminuendo. The smoke has cleared, the dead lie still, the god has granted victory. All is well, in heaven as on earth. Or so it is implied.

~

To military chaplains, to football players and their coaches, from the tragic to the frivolous, the story of the intercessor, arms outstretched and supported, together with the celestial response, might indeed be thought "witness to the efficacy of prayer."

Perhaps an episode from the life of Jesus offers a corrective. On the eve of his passion and death, he retires to prayer in the garden of Gethsemane.

In these words:

> Father,
> if it is
> your will,
>
> take this cup
> from me;
>
> yet not my will
> but yours
>
> be
> done . . .
>
> In anguish
> he prayed
> with greater intensity,
>
> and his sweat
> became
> like drops of blood
>
> falling
> to
> ground. (Luke 22:42; Luke 22:44)

Context is everything. Jesus perseveres in prayer. It might be adduced by way of simile that he, too, faces a battle. In prelude to the contest, his spirit wrestles with the shadowy angel. Anguish explodes in the silence; capillaries are opened and blood falls.

What differences here! The "battle" of Jesus is of the spirit; shall he be required to give his life on the morrow? And if so, for whose sake, and to whose benefit?

The blood that falls to ground is—His own. No persecutors, Pilate, Herod, soldiers, executioners, are at risk. He alone is at risk. An anguished prospect fells Him. What must be let be. Freedom is reduced to this: Your will, not mine.

~

What bitter contrast, what a totally other world is opened by the prayer of Moses. The hope that governs his prayer, that keeps his arms aloft, is a dream of victory for the chosen. This together with the larger scene, the murderous valor of Joshua, the fog and blood and night falling.

And those "enemies of the chosen"—who are they? In a time of sanity, they would be seen as a multitude of youths, of farmers and artisans and spouses and parents, merchants, day laborers, students. Humans connected one to another by affection and blood.

~

The Mosaic scene, alas, is hardly to be thought sane. A murderous battle is underway. The actors, whether named or anonymous, are transformed, as though in a nightmare by day. Moses at prayer, Joshua dim in the fray—and soldiers of the chosen, killing and dying.

And the enemy. Let his fate (along with the fate of the Hebrew casualties-to-be) count as nothing. As if they were not. Nameless, with no story to tell, to weep for.

Keep to the main chance! Moses prays, Joshua fights, Yahweh hearkens.

Must someone die; must many die? The question is beside the point.

~

Let us have recourse, for sanity's sake, to an exegesis that summons our great midrash of compassion and remembering.

"For the duration" of the sacred battle, Jesus is absent from the academic commentary. Absent? More exactly, He is evicted.

No saving, sane contrast. Christian scholars ignore Him, "for the duration."

"The [Mosaic] episode is cited as witness to the efficacy of prayer."

~

Also of small matter (or none at all), the prayer known as the Lord's own. And its petition for untrammeled commerce between heaven and earth, that in the sublime act of pardoning, earth comes to resemble heaven:

> Forgive us
> our debts,
>
> as
> we also
>
> have
> forgiven
>
> our
> debtors . . . (Matt 6:12)

In truth, that prayer, too, were best put to one side, "for the duration" of this or that war. Rather, let this be intoned: "Onward, Christian soldiers!"

~

We make our way as best we might through the text. It becomes a welter, a blur of war, a mad canvas entitled *Guérnica*. Amid the slaughter, helpers are at hand; the god of battles, together with pious intercessors, and the sword of a military wizard. Thus the chosen and their god prevail.

~

The Catholic chaplain at the former School of the Americas at Fort Benning, Georgia, defended the school against charges that torture was taught there, that every Latin dictator and general had graduated from its ranks:

The School has been very carefully scrutinized by our own gov-
ernment, and was cleared of wrongdoing. . . . My parish council
has included former SOA faculty members and its chief of staff.
These are just profoundly decent, committed lay men and women
who would have nothing to do with a place that was doing something tawdry or wrong or immoral . . . We share our methodol-
ogy and our military doctrine and try to learn something from
them. We also make a point of sharing our democratic traditions,
helping them understand how a military operates under civilian
control in a democracy.[23]

—*Catholic News Service, "Washington Letter"*

Enough said.

~

Verses 14–16

So our text inducts us into the reality of "holy war." And its immediate
(and remote) consequence as well.

A victory is won. And a message from Yahweh includes a dual command. The memory of the foe must be blotted out and an altar raised in
commemoration of the "holy" prevailing.

This god, we have noted before, is endowed with a perduring, highly
selective memory. Not only are good and great occasions to be commem-
orated, but (if one can so speak), he "remembers to forget" the opposite,
the bad and the lesser.

~

An altogether curious, brutal form of scapegoating is underway. In the
text, we must traverse a wilderness of moral waste and want—in this deity, in ourselves.

Until you, prophets, and You, Jesus, lead us out.

~

Meantime, in the awful meantime that defines the Mosaic era, the warrior mind is socialized and raised to the empyrean, to heaven. The warrior, as such, is consecrated to the deity; thus, the iron supposition. War
is a godly calling; it is the will of the god.

And enmities endure as long as time lasts; this by empyrean decree: "Yahweh is in battle against Amalek through the centuries" (Exod 17:16).

~

 From the battles of Exodus, imperialism emerges. It is a cannibal ideology and practice. It flourishes on the flesh of corpses. And the deity ("its" deity), brooding over the battlefield, takes joy in "victory." (And what, one asks, of the mentality that requires, creates, celebrates, such a deity?)

The perdurance of conflict is a decree of heaven, of the deity. A superhuman agent is at work, quite taken for granted. Earthly enmities are granted a divine sanction; the wars of the chosen are not only just, they are blessed, holy. Against forgiveness, conversion of heart, reconciling—the eternal has set his shoulder like a wall.

~

We see the consequence of this down the centuries, this bizarre sanctioning of death, we humans stuck in the Realm of Necessity. And spawned of that necessity, a theology "from above" flourishes; a god of armed might, of "just wars."

"God of power and might," we intone. The god is revealed as "standing above."

Our humankind is likewise revealed as the tribe of Cain, not of Abel. Until Christ, and the blood of Abel vindicated.

~

" . . . and even this is only half a revenge." And what is the other half?

Let us invoke the midrash devised by Christ. That "other half" is the sweet revenge of Christ, His plucking from the hands of Cain the brute symbols of the fallen, the club and sword.

The sweet revenge, for our sake; that we might stand under the tutelage of different metaphors and ikons.

The tribe of Cain has passed into the hands of his brother Abel. Now our vocation must be thought, against all odds, the 'raising of Abel'.

~

EXODUS 18

Verses 1–12

We are favored with a rare family encounter of this most public man, Moses. Details of the story are left to our imagining: how, for safety's sake, Moses had sent wife and sons from Egypt, back to her people in Midian. That land, it will be remembered (Exod 2:22) was a place of both exile and refuge for young Moses; there he found his bride and started a family.

~

Tenderness, ties of the heart—these would seem all but forgotten in the life of the liberator. At last they are summoned here, and vividly celebrated.

The author turns us about, fascinated, under the magic of his mood. The smoke of battle has cleared. And we are led from clash of arms to a scene fragrant with tenderness and immediacy.

For a while, the worst is in the past tense. Frowns clear, smiles appear on the face of day. The scene is bathed in serene joy as father-in-law, Jethro, conducts the bride and sons to a reunion with Moses in the desert. Embraces, inquiries as to the health of each.

Together, the family enters the tent. Talk and more talk. Moses has wonders to relate, the mighty works of God, the plagues and their outcome, the favor of God's own. Thus, the story is passed on, warts and all, the god of blessings, the rejecting god, the game, winners and losers.

The sons are attentive, all ears, these youthful partisans of the next chapter of life. And toward evening the stories are validated with worship and sacrifice and a great banquet.

~

And for ourselves? We taste a rare sweetness; more, we are summoned ever so subtly—or perhaps not so subtly—to take sides, to stand with this gigantic figure: forerunner; prophet; lawgiver; mystic; spouse, and father. This tender strong one, in reunion with his loved ones. Who could resist him?

Then a caution, a midrash. A fire is lighted in the tent; it casts deep shadows, stirs second thoughts and a critique.

The bloodline, the family tie, is one thing, laudable to be sure. But what of the enemy? Does the enemy also hold precious ties with spouse and children? Does the enemy gather with his own? Is his story of valor and love recorded and told somewhere?

~

It is a terrible thought (and a contemporary horror as well). In our story, it tightens like a noose. This: Moses is a tribal being, servant of a tribal god.

So, are we Americans to be accounted tribal, in this year, in this millennium, in this war. The boundaries of affection, of cherishing and protecting, are drawn in blood, a closed circle. The nation; first, foremost, sole, privileged.

What of the "outsiders"? On them the tribe casts a cold eye. The children of Iraq are weighed in the scales of Mars, judged expendable, and disposed of. So, beyond doubt, are the children of Afghanistan.

There could be no more terrible evidence of a reeking inhumanity.

~

And in face of this,

> My command
> to you
>
> is
> this;
>
> love
> your enemies,
>
> pray
> for
> your
> persecutors. (Matt 6:44)

And this,

> . . . His mother
> and his brothers

appeared outside
to speak with him.

Someone
said to him,

"your mother
and your brothers

are standing
out there

and they wish
to speak to you."

He said,

"who
is my mother,

who
are my brothers?"

Then
extending his hand

toward his disciples,
he said,

"these are
my mother
and my brothers.

Whoever
does the will
of my heavenly father

is

brother

and

sister

and

mother

to

me." (Matt 12:46–50)

~

Verses 13–27

Warrior Jethro is a canny second in command. He takes note of a typical day in the life of Moses. Appalling: morning to night the great man is overwhelmed with a crush of litigants—plaintiffs and defendants. Each brings a burden and casts it at the feet of Moses.

As often as not, the contentions are laced with caprice and ill will.

Impossible, draining. There must be a better way. For sake of greater causes, Moses must be granted relief: here, now, on the foothills of destiny, our leader must not be exhausted with small coins flung at him.

Sinai beckons. Jethro is insistent. Let us fashion a system of relief, organize, delegate. Let the day-by-day, small-claim courts be presided over by

"capable, godfearing, trustworthy, incorruptible men *[sic]*" chosen for this duty.

And Moses? Let him restrict himself to the office of mediator,

"the people's representative before God" (Exod 18:19),

and of instructor,

"showing them how they are to live, how to conduct themselves" (Exod 18:20).

Thus, through Jethro, the first institution of the exodus, that of the judges, is set in place. The arrangement will prove durable. After the settlement in Canaan, it will be canonized. And, eventually riven with nepotism and greed, the judges will fall before the onset of the monarchy.

~

EXODUS 19

Verse 1 and following

So, we come to one of the great theophanies of our book, indeed of the entire Bible. Moses is famously summoned to the heights of Sinai, for "forty days and nights," there to be wrapped in the cloud of unknowing.

And the people? They are warned; *"procul este; stand afar!"* (Exod 19:12).

Nature is shaken. The elements bespeak crisis, eruption, birth pangs, thunder, lightning, promulgation of law, ecstasies, a charged air of commerce between earth and heaven.

~

In unraveling the events, it might be of help to concentrate on the self-revelation of Yahweh:

—A general rule seems to apply, a law of ironies compounded. Through our omniscient storyteller, we accompany Moses up the mountain and approach the Mystery. The consummate privilege is denied the plebs. For a time, access to the Epiphany is forbidden elders as well.

—Even as crisis grows, we note this: the Presence takes the form of cloud, thunders, wind, lightnings, a voice. As the deity nears, the ironies and contradictions multiply, intensify.

—On the mountain, Yahweh is pleased to open an eye, to see and be seen. That eye is fierce as the eye of a storm. He is pure vortex, he dwells in a cave whence all storms emerge.

—Or this: nothing of the above holds true. The deity is pleased to show another mood entirely.

What mood? We shall see.

~

The first encounter between the god and Moses hardly prepares us for what is to follow. We witness a monologue, somewhat iffy, a prelude to the proclaiming of the decalogue.

The instruction is enveloped in tenderness and promise:

You
shall be

a realm of

priests,

a

holy

nation. (Exod 19:6)

And yet another *if*. The divine favor includes a codicil, a stern one. The chosen must choose; obey and prosper, rebel and be destroyed.

We shall see the theme developed throughout the wilderness years, on to Canaan and the glory days of Solomon.

And likewise in the times of sore critique and naysaying, as the prophets arise, those raging critics of "things as they are."

~

Self-revealed in this place, vulnerable despite the pyrotechnics in nature, the decor of omnipotence—Yahweh is strangely a prisoner to his own law. The law forbids the welling up of spontaneous love.

Shall the heart of the deity show? A *despite* impedes; the delicts, grievous and successive, of his tribe.

~

Verse 9 and following

Forty days? But that, it would seem, is a human calculation, arbitrary. While Moses is enveloped in the divinity, time falls to chaos. Days pass or do not, Yahweh dwells in a vast timelessness, overruling, even canceling, the human calendar.

And of Moses, it is as though he were gifted with a kind of bilocation. Now he is aloft, again he rejoins his own below.

A triduum of cleansing is commanded. The people are agog with preparation for an epiphany—an event that formerly excluded them under pain of death.

Now, a sea change. The event will include (even as it sets limits to) communal access.

~

In another version, the deity shows an elite, somewhat finical mood. Moses, Aaron, the elders, form a tight circle of those permitted approach.

As for "the people"—what of them? They are regarded as variously uninstructed, unworthy, unclean, of a lingering half-Egyptian appetite and mind (those fleshpots, that golden calf on the horizon!). The judgment; they are in dire need of discipline.

By strong implication (the closed circle, the distancing, the intercessors), there are hierarchies, degrees of "being chosen."

In this version, the deity on the heights is marked by an olympian distain, a distrust of the common herd.

~

Verse 16

Comes the day of days. After the 'son et lumiere,' the decor of majesty unapproachable—the moment. It is recorded simply, directly. The narrative is a stroke of genius, plain and pointed.

We, too, are invited to join the procession en route to a fuller humanity:

> Moses
> led
> the people
>
> out
> of the camp
>
> to
> meet
> God.

~

Yes, but . . . To meet the god indeed, but from afar. Death is in the air, it hovers over, the crepuscular other name of that luminous Cloud.

A law governs the present version. Does one dare approach near? If so, the threat of reprisal mounts.

You would come near? Risk then an "unchoosing," the dismantling of the promise. The threat: you shall die.

A concession is made to the priests; perhaps they may come a bit closer. . . . But let these take care, only the pure need apply!

> Else
>> he will vent
>
>> his
> anger
>
> upon
> them! (Exodus 19:22)

As for lesser mortals—none among the people is to mount.

>> . . . warn
> the people
>
> not
> to break through
>
>> to
> the Lord
>
>> in order
> to see him;
>
>> otherwise
>> many
> of them
> will
> be
>
> struck
> down. (Exod 19:21)

~

Perplexity. Why this vast threat, the insistence on every jot and tittle of protocol? And strangest of all, the anger sputtering away like a charge timed for explosion? Can the unthinkable be true, that the omnipotent is strangely vulnerable, unsure? Are the rubrics of distance and access a kind of cloud cover, behind which dwells a god uncertain of his throne?

~

EXODUS 20

Without further ado, onto a bare stage, comes the supreme moment of visionary time. It would seem likely (but this is at best implied) that the decalogue is issued to Moses and Aaron only, the two enveloped in the cloud.

First, as we say, the promise, sweetening the *sine qua non* of law. Then the law. Yahweh, as we have suggested, is also held to it, a Prometheus in bonds. Bound to the threat, as to the promise.

> only
> if you
>
> are
> faithful,
>
> otherwise . . . (Exod 20:24–25)

~

An anthropology is being devised. It is like the molding of another Adam.

Is this version of the human definitive, final? So it seemed at the time, but what surprises are in store! We are told that it is set in stone. But even stone falls to dust.

And that new version, that "humanity"—its lineaments are in immemorial flux. Its nearest image is this setting, this pause at the foot of a mountain, and a desert pilgrimage shortly to be resumed.

The version offered here, legislated solemnly—time will show it true, firm, noble, marvelously validated and embodied in saints and prophets and martyrs.

Often as well, defaulted on—even, in sordid practice, denied.

≈

Verse 23 and following

In view of an abomination shortly to follow, we take note of one item of the "law of the altar":

Do not

make
anything

to rank
with me;

neither gods
of silver

nor gods
of gold

shall you
make

for
yourselves. (Exod 20:2)

Indeed.

Exodus 21–34

EXODUS 21-23

Herein are offered, and in quelling detail, rules of communal and personal ethic. (And not once but twice; the same will be repeated toward the end of our Exodus book.)

Sections of the legislation reflect a later period, pointing to the end of the desert sojourn, and the settlements in Canaan. We note allusions to dwellings, to beasts of burden, to labor in fields and vineyards. The wanderers are claiming the land; their code is being adapted to a society of shepherds and peasants.

~

Simply put, these chapters elaborate the decalogue, somewhat clumsily, with more or less conscious borrowing from other codes of the same era.

But the decalogue itself is another matter. Its bare bones are incandescent with new life. According to some commentators, it anticipates accurately the preaching of later prophets. If so, a (muted) alleluia.

~

Like spelunkers in semidarkness, we halt in wonderment: layer upon layer of accumulation, hints, textures—bones of the holy ones, sketches on the walls—that splendid undimmed tradition!

And then a final "sifting of soil," the redaction before us.

And the great prophets arise. Do not their noble bones grow animate and lead us on, all but speaking aloud to us?

~

EXODUS 24

Verses 1–11

Two traditions are brought to bear in the episode of the sealing of covenant. In one, atop the mountain, a banquet or picnic is attended by a few chosen. In the other, blood sacrifice is celebrated in presence of everyone, at the foot of the mountain.

Let us linger over the first (vv 1 and 2; vv 9–11) as by far the most spectacular, even daring—and perhaps the original version? One hopes so!

This occurs. Moses and friends and relatives, together with seventy elders, climb up. Then something unprecedented—an event shakes the creation, more wondrous than a bush afire.

A Someone appears:

They
beheld

the
God

of
Israel.

Simple, unadorned as that. No description, no imagery. How could there be description or imagery?

A Someone. And a setting:

under
his feet

there
appeared
to be

sapphire
tile
work,

as clear

as

the

sky

itself. (Exod 24:10)

In a strange reversal of "below and "above," the "tile work" is "under his feet"; it is also "clear as the sky." Is this what happens when mortals see God—does the universe suddenly lose its moorings, turn topsy-turvy, the sky no longer stretching above, but underfoot, under the feet of—God?

Under the feet of mortals?

The god, too, turns and turns about. By thunderous words often reiterated, such as these elders were once threatened with death on the spot.

No more of that. Mightily, and unexpectedly, the god restrains himself.

The elders were invited up the mountain (v. 1), but Moses alone was allowed to approach the deity; the elders were warned; not too close!

They came perilously near. And they survived.

And more, how much more! We are privy to an unprecedented outcome.

There on the mount of revelation, in a cloud bristling with terrors, the deity draws close. And mortal danger dissolves. The fury is transmogrified. And so are the daring ones. The god of terror plays host; humans are his guests. Together they sit to a picnic!

They

looked

at

God

and

they

ate

and

drank. (Exod 24:11)

~

A breakthrough? The mind stutters. Make of it what one will.

This might be ventured; a Presence is widening its embrace, broadening mortal access to a once-inviolate Self. Others than Moses are being favored.

Still, we note that an elite is implied; in neither account are the people invited to behold, to "eat and drink."

~

A comparison, a midrash. Were one to soften the staging and atmosphere of our scene on the mountain, tumultuous as it is—the serene, intimate banquet might bring to mind a scene toward the end of John's Gospel.

Dawn breaks, and Jesus appears on the lakeshore. He has prepared a breakfast of fish. No lightning bolts, no threats. Not so much as a reproof to those who, a few days before, fled the scene of His death.

Instead, a welcome and early morning hospitality offered the weary. Half-bewildered, more than half (at long last!) believing, the fishermen sit to a meal hosted by the risen One, this unprecedented Master of vanishings and epiphanies (John 21:1–14).

~

Verses 12–18

Finally, on Mount Sinai the stone tablets are bestowed. And once more we read two versions of the tale, uneasily joined.

The writing down of law, its "setting in stone," is an ancient custom, we are told. It gave permanence and dignity to whatever decrees. (The law of Hammurabi, for instance, was famously engraved on a tall stele).

Moses climbs up to receive the promised tablets. But first, he issues instructions. With a mind, perhaps, of reducing the possibility of another communal default (how that golden calf rankles!). Subtly Aaron is reminded; in my absence, you are responsible for good order in the rank and file.

Then he ascends. The tablets, for the moment, are ignored. For a period of time—or of timelessness—Moses is swept into the *shekinah*.

~

EXODUS 25

A grandiose fusion of events here. As though looking back over his shoulder, the historian views the Ark and the Tent, those humble dwellings of the holy, from the lofty vantage of the Solomonic temple.

He presents the history of worship as a vast complex mosaic. Its first images are quite modest, as befit a people on the move.

~

In our book of Exodus, the Tent and Ark occupy a minor place. Still, the genius of the chronicler joins time present to time future. Eventually, it is implied, the humble tabernacle yields to the great temple. The two are one—if not in form, in equal honor to the "One who is."

~

The Ark, we are told, was a large, ornately carven box. It contained in a golden vase the memorial manna (that marvelous prototype of the blessed sacrament of Christians), together with the stone tablets of the law, named by Yahweh, the "Witness."

Sign and surety of the presence of Yahweh, after the event of Mount Horeb, the Ark became the safeguard of Israel. Wherever the people went, the Ark went before, borne on poles of acacia wood. At a bivouac in the desert or an oasis inviting an overnight halt, the Ark was deposited in an airy tent, easily set up and disassembled.

~

Like colored stones in their setting, history is fused; converging, splendid, mysterious. What a mosaic of event and intervention, the pilgrimage that begins here!

The path, the years of wandering, meander on and on, an image of universal history, of sin and divagation of every sort and sordidness. Under the arcane gaze of our author, no dark act, no willful omission is withheld or censored. For better and worse, humanity is on the march—our communal story.

Thus the landmarks, seamarks of the exodus: the desert, the sea crossing, the modest tent and sacred paraphernalia, the forty years of hither and yon, the miraculous food and drink, the merciless chastisements. In the wilderness, an entire generation is forbidden entrance to the promise, and perishes.

Those who departed Egypt were judged and found wanting, freed from slavery only to fall short, condemned by a god, terrible and implacable as the pharaoh. Multitudes perish in the desert.

Then the subsequent centuries, a trail of blood and tears: the promise of the kings; a fair start shattered by dark Saul; rendered ambiguous by David; restored for a time by a wise, compassionate Solomon. Not for long.

The overbearing architecture of empire rises, the imperial system grows carnivorous, and the king capitulates to selfishness, greed, wars and alarums.

~

Does one long (rightfully, wrongly?) for a less awful story, a less impure religion? Before our eyes, alas, stands this story and no other. Our own. Our ancestry: a chronicle of sinners and saints, of the godly and demonic, of a few heroic ones clinging to hope, of others death-ridden, deceitful, betraying.

Some are born to embody the promise, to redeem evil times: the saints and prophets and martyrs, their witness to the truth—unto death, if so it must be.

We make of it what we will. We confess, this is the truth of our lot, our passage in the world. We recognize, and submit. Or we turn away in disgust and disbelief.

But to what alternative? To America?

~

Beyond doubt, we have at hand other, ideologically loaded versions of ancestry. Huckstered by this or that culture, these stories of beginnings are all light, virtue, glory.

Does God write straight with crooked lines? So it is anciently said. And so it is denied implicitly today by media and politicos and tycoons, by those who contrive and huckster the ambiguous matrix of myth.

In current American culture, the god has a less exacting task; he *[sic]* need not straighten the lines of history. No eventuality, no "long view" is required. From the start, the lines are straight as arrows launched by olympian archers. By ourselves.

~

Exodus might seem, in contrast, a story written in shifty sand, a tale easily obliterated by desert winds.

And it is not obliterated, not a jot or tittle, to our own day. We wonder and surmise. Shall there be a final "straightening out" of the lines that start here, in the seemingly aimless arc of desert nomads, their forty years of meandering?

What prospect kept the heart of Moses steady? Only a long view, a hope that hoped on, could summon, despite all, a favorable outcome. The Promise, the Promise—cry it into contrary winds, though few give ear!

~

The judges were established, as we have seen. The chosen arrived and won the land. Then a clamor arose, *Give us a king!*

Despite many a reservation on the part of Samuel, the god and his seer yielded. Great names emerged, the era of glory was underway: Saul, David, Solomon, Hezekiah. Meantime, and with increasing vehemence, internal divisions, assassinations, chicanery, betrayal. And the two kingdoms split like a rotten fruit.

Bathos, that ending; no bang, a whimper. The story peters out with the decline and fall of Solomon, the accession of Hezekiah, followed by a series of royal puppets.

~

And a question, inevitably: Is the history of the chosen to be thought morally superior to, say, the gods of the tribes of Canaan? Of these latter our Bible offers no story; they fall nameless, soundless, like a great tree in an uninhabited forest. Rather than their story (and more awful by far), we have an account of the sanctified righteousness of those who destroyed them.

~

EXODUS 26-30

A garden of minutiae thrives in these chapters. Let us grant the liturgists, those exquisite horticulturists, free play amid the weeds and roses, a garden of starry instruction!

We are also in a double helix of time. Back, forth, in text and time, the seeing eye must voyage. For the nonce, the time is of exodus; the worship and its accoutrements are simplicity itself: the Tent, the Ark.

But then a tumble of centuries, and we are catapulted forward. Intimations of grandeur rise like a perfume from the text; it is as though in a haze of time the towers of Jerusalem appeared.

Is this a desert mirage? We rub our eyes; the priests have wrought magic. The tradition is transformed; now it is firmly sacerdotal. Instructions abound: the Tent and its wooden walls, the Ark, the Table of Oblation, the Court, the Oil. Elaborations testify. The exodus has ended; the wanderers have planted roots in Canaan.

And their fortunes have expanded wonderfully: an imperium is set in stone.

Priests enter the text in royal procession, pristine and glorious. Worship is stately, self-confident, consciously reclaiming (read: reshaping) the past. With a bias of pridefulness, out of meager scrolls and bits and pieces of oral memory, with what skill and labor the story is assembled!

An ineluctable logic comes in play. If necessary, let the past be altered in favor of the ideology of empire, a past found worthy of the sheen and shimmer of present grandeur.

~

Clerical assurance staggers the mind. Choice and outcome were providential from the start; all was ordained from on high, anciently decreed, then set in stone. Again and again, the instruction begins with an inviolate formula:

Yahweh

spoke

to

Moses

and

said

to

him . . . .

Our attention is puzzled. Is this the accurate image—Yahweh, enveloped in a brooding cloud, a cloud like an all-seeing eye, the deity reading aloud to his Moses, from detailed notes set down by seraphs?

Would the famous forty days and nights suffice to assemble this splendid verbal mosaic, every stone agleam?

~

According to the priesthood, the god of the *shekinah* is suffused with imperial longings. To this god the line of David inhabits a veritable heaven on earth. The empire! The praise swells and rises to this apogee; the Davidic system is the ultimate social and political form of assembled humans. Heavenly Jerusalem, the holy city! No wonder the god is pleased to be borne homeward, to dwell in the splendid temple of Solomon.

Dare one say it? The god has all but said it. David and his like have repaired the Fall.

~

A later poet ruminates, and doubts. He walks about Jerusalem, solitary. The ground under his feet is a bone meal of centuries. Indeed, doubts are a speaking rubble that counsels, Look about you, to this has glory come.

Doubts, another image. They are the common twilight; in it, we and the poet walk. Nothing final, not even rubble.

~

David takes his harp to sing the glories of Yahweh. Felicitations waft through his strings. Clearly, the mood is reciprocated. The deity is an ideal overlord, wonderfully selective in conscience, a moving front of power and might, a god whose purpose prevails in the world, by whatever means. And the prevailing—altogether in favor of his royal darling, David.

Reciprocity, dovetailing! The god has decreed this as well; the imperial tribe of David will prevail in the world—and by whatever means.

Has not the god, for the sake of the prospering of his favorites, sanctioned—nay commanded—the anathema, the wars of "take no prisoners, spare no living beings"?

~

We live after the fact; even in our sorry skulls, time has lodged a seed of wisdom.

There follows in due time the decline and fall of the house of David. Could we not apply to the catastrophe, the threnody of the great angel of Revelation, witnessing the toppling of Babylon?

> Fallen, fallen
> is Babylon
> the great!
>
> She
> has become
>
> a dwelling place
> for demons,
>
> a cage
> for
> every
>
> unclean
> spirit . . . (Rev 18:2)

Alas for the grand days, the psalmody and processions, the stringed instruments, the incense and chanting and dance, the reek of blood at the altar! The cloud, for all its glory, is tinged with sunset, the hectic scarlet and ochre of decline, just before darkness takes the earth for Dis.

~

The priests solemnly issue from the womb of time, composing their story, eloquent as it is—and exigent, as well, of due honors and perquisites.

Confidently they speak on behalf of the god who sees beyond mortal ken, who sees the end time and consecrates it to himself. Of that time the priests, holy, sumptuous—and doomed—are the appointed guardian spirits. So declares Yahweh. Or so the priests declare that the god declares.

∾

EXODUS 31

Verses 12–18

Finally, as a kind of liturgical climax, an instruction is issued. The preceding minutiae would seem to stand as a kind of rehearsal. The curtain rises; sabbath observance is the drama itself, solemn, full-bodied, publicly staged.

∾

The imposition of sabbath rest has no apparent link with the preceding. We have here an independent law, inserted by an editor who would highlight the meaning of sabbath in the cult.

∾

In any case, the command is issued sternly: a death threat hangs over violators. And we are chastened; lethal legislation implies the seriousness with which Yahweh takes himself. An analogy is set in place, as though in stone; "it (the sabbath) is an unbreakable covenant." The analogy? During six days, humans are busy about their works. This is their dignity; to mime and to be reminded of the works of the creator. And on the seventh day God rests; and so do we. This too is in tribute to our dignity, that we "enter the cloud," a contrasting rhythm, due need paid to hungers of soul and spirit.

∾

Enough. To a summary. The interminable "forty days and nights" are ended. Moses staggers into human day, trailing clouds of glory. He bears in hand the stony tablets of divine will, *pondus gloriae*, a "burden of glory," as Paul will have it (Rom 8:18).

Oxymoronic—and how could it be otherwise, this divine-human commerce signified and sealed in stone?

We marvel. Daring to the end, with style and sting the priest-scribe writes his *finis*. Take it or leave.

But if you leave, beware. The divine credential is one with the priestly. The tablets are inscribed "by the finger of God."

∾

EXODUS 32

We recall that before his ascent, Moses left Aaron in charge of judicial matters below (Exod 24:14). Now a neat intercalation as we turn to events at the foot of the mountain.

In the camp, trouble is brewing, fiercely. The sojourn of Moses aloft seems interminable. Wrapped on the mountain, has he abandoned his own? Bereft and restless, the people approach Aaron. They know (or the author knows; it comes to the same.) that in time of crisis, the "nations," whether Assyrian or Egyptian, expose and venerate images of their gods. So why not for ourselves, a god to guard us in this rudderless interim?

∾

A warning signal, one surmises, conveyed as though over the shoulder of a later time, from the era of Solomon's temple-god, back and back, to an awful event in the desert years.

Too little, too late? Out of the imperium comes this gift of sad wisdom. It issues from a blank liturgy, a priesthood sold to venality, a people busy about worldly works and pomps, the commerce and wars of Solomon. In Jerusalem, each is a grim index of decline and fall.

∾

One implication among many—disaster took its start here, in the desert, at the foot of the mount of revelation. Dare venture it; the golden calf portends the great temple. In this view, a small idol engenders a vast one. The prophets will shout it abroad, most vociferously Ezekiel, *the temple is an idol!* (Ezekiel 8–9).

~

In the desert default, Aaron, and Moses himself, are implicated from the start. Confusion reigns, perhaps of purpose. Is Moses commanded to collect the gold ornaments, perhaps (or perhaps not) in view of their firing (Exod 33:5–6)? Or does Aaron take the initiative (Exod 32:2–3) with the melding of the notorious calf? And that ambiguous image, what to make of it? Does it represent Yahweh (as in Exod 32:5) or a rival god (as in Exod 32:26)?

Our storyteller draws on scraps of tradition, stitches them together, masterfully ambiguous. As in every tale well told, much is left to ourselves.

For instance, note this implication of the story: in some way or another, were not the brothers, Moses and Aaron, partners in decisions that border on the heinous? And the golden image—is it not to be judged dangerous (in view of surrounding idolatries) as well as ambiguous (in view of the great temple to come)?

And what of the god and his part in the episode? This at least is clear: the deity is near and witnesses all—even, truth told, nudges the action forward.

~

Verses 15 and following

Moses at long last descends. The scene in the valley has erupted in a vortex of revelry and worship.

The seer explodes in fury. The tablets of the decalogue fall—better, are hurled to ground. The calf is pulled down and ground to a powder.

An accounting is inevitable. Elaborate verbal niceties are spun as Aaron seeks to justify himself. His rejoinder is astonishing: he is wide-eyed with innocence, covert, equivocal, empty of remorse. *The people,* he insists, *it was the people who led me. Not astray—no such thing. Let us say only—they led me to do what I did.*

And what did Aaron do?

The indictment: *You were complicit; you surely know*
"how prone the people are to evil" (Exod 32:22).
The retort: *Nothing of this.*
"I asked them, "who among you possesses gold?" They stripped themselves, I threw the gold in the fire, and this calf came out!" (Exod 32:24).

Aaron might be describing a bovine birth in a Canaanite barn: "this calf came out." Country matters, nothing more; the words are larded with feigned innocence, sunk in nature.

Then the curious outcome; in heaven as on earth, nepotism wins the day. On the instant, the delict is forgiven or forgotten, or both.

∾

Still, a question: Was the deed of Aaron a delict, or an initiative of true worship? Was the image to be thought an idol or an image of true god? The text veers wildly.

Has Aaron failed only venially, has he "let the people run wild" (Exod 32:25)? Or has he "delivered them into idolatry" (Exod 32:5, 8, 31)? Both are proposed. In any case, the outcome is astonishing. An ambiguous argument satisfies both his brother and the god; Aaron will endure no consequence, undergo no punishment. How could he, justly? is the implication.

∾

Verse 6

An orgy, we are told, has followed on the worship;
"... they sat to eat and drink and rose to play."
The outcome is pure terror, a bloodbath, initiated by Moses. And this even as brother walks free.

Speedily, ruin gathers, human bonds are sundered. The Levites are brought to the fore, and bare their swords. By decree of Yahweh (in this version mortally offended), an order is issued. No trial, no evidence, no defense allowed. You, Levites, slaughter whom you will, be it brother, friend, neighbor.

∾

But . . .

> Let the one who is intent on vengeance dig two graves.
>
> —*Chinese proverb*

∽

This orgy of another sort—of divine jealousy! Obedient to the decree, the Levites are rewarded with the laurels of priesthood.

 Surely we are witnesses to a curious form of justice, implying a large omission. What of Aaron and the molten image? A wave of the hand, whether of Moses's hand or Yahweh's, and the brother's case is dismissed. By decision of heaven and earth (each domain susceptible to special interests), the behavior of Aaron is declared a peccadillo, a yielding before popular pressure.

∽

And what, in light of the above, is one to make of the following, surely a curious twist of casuistry?

> " . . . he did turn many away from iniquity" (Mal 2:6). What means "did turn many away from iniquity"? When Aaron walked along the street and met a wicked man, he gave him greeting. The next day, when that person wanted to commit a transgression, he would say to himself, "How can I after doing such an act, lift up my eyes and look at Aaron? I should feel ashamed before him who gave me greeting." As a consequence, he would refrain from doing wrong.
>
> Similarly when two men were at enmity with one another, Aaron would visit one of them and say to him, "My son, see how your friend is behaving; he beats his breast, tears his garment and cries, 'Woe is me, how can I look into the face of my friend? I am ashamed before him, since it was I who acted shabbily toward him!'"
>
> Aaron would continue to sit with him until he had banished all enmity from his heart. Then he went and spoke exactly the same words to the other party, until he had removed all enmity from him. The result was that when the two men met, they embraced and kissed one another.[24]
>
> —*Everyman's Talmud*

~

EXODUS 33

For eleven months the caravan pauses at Sinai (Num 10:11–13). Then a command, a mélange of promise and threat: Move on!

Those in possession of Canaan will, as previously announced, be "driven out" (Exod 33:2). That prophecy holds firm.

Still, with regard to the chosen, there is no forgetting recent delicts. The tone of the deity turns ominous; lightnings of the mountaintop linger on the air. You, survivors of wrath, be warned (Exod 33:3)! The god's memory is a bared Excalibur. Ironically, he warns; there will be no warning.

To put matters clumsily, the god could not trust himself not to slaughter them along the way. So abiding is his anger, seething in secret, a kind of underground fire surfacing here, there, anywhere.

Somehow the deity must contain himself. Lest he renew the recent slaughter, he will send a substitute as guardian and guide, an angel (33:2).

Meantime, as sign of remorse, they are to remove from their persons all precious ornaments. The stripping will remove a close temptation—to make of such trinkets another meltdown abomination (Exod 33:6).

~

One thinks of the subtext here: deep, helpful—and unsettling. On the face of it, the calf story offered a rather childish episode. To wit: in the protracted absence of a father figure, an oracle and mediator, the people cast gold into an ambiguous image. Whose image, the right god, the wrong one? Whose offense? Certainly not Aaron's—or so it is adduced.

But . . . but . . . Many must pay. In a showcase execution, multitudes are punished, a bloody tat for a golden tit. Thus, the god strikes out, reestablishing his (shaky?) sovereignty.

The deity knows their hearts, knows how likely is a repetition of the outrage. So they must remove pendant, bracelets, rings, amulets, necklaces, anklets, all the booty lifted from the goy slave masters. Displayed, such will serve only to occasion further delicts.

~

How tempting (one thinks) to distance ourselves from the story, primitive as it may be judged, preadolescent even. Let us (pace Aaron and his presumed innocence) for a moment presuppose that the worst occurred—an episode of idolatry in the desert.

And we dare reflect on ourselves, on our culture. We Americans, too, are skilled in the casting of idols, a bestiary of idols, technologically innovative, masked as to intent and form, self-justifying, mortally dangerous. And yet befitting (as perversely seems) a lofty status in the world.

Our idols are deaf, dumb, blind, the "works of our hands"; gods of appetite and domination—smart bombs tipped with depleted uranium; fleets of bombers, submarines, destroyers—angels of the last day patrolling waters, skies, lands, outer space; threatening, where they do not already wreak, havoc of creation.

Idolatry, in sum, imbedded in a culture that (according to its own canons of political, military, religious correctness) has "come of age."

Who will heal us of this mortal willfulness? We have cast in an atomic furnace, emblems of pride and violence, in view of the molding of a monstrous baal.

~

Verses 7–11

The ideology of the Solomonic empire tolerates a god of lightnings and olympian furore. But only, be it noted, as an episode, only for a time. The priests are canny; a wild tradition must be mollified if the empire is to flourish under a pennant of law and order—law and order in Jerusalem, if not in the heavens!

A reminder might be helpful once more; our text is deep in a time warp. Here and now, in the Sinaitic desert in the twelfth century BCE, amid a wandering tribe, the deity calms down; the god of the tent preempts the wild Lear of the mountain.

Our account is assembled later by a cadre of true believers ensconced in the great temple. Centuries have come and gone; the god has learned the *nil nimis* ("nothing extreme"), the *aurea media* ("golden mean") motto of a deity who serves, even as he *[sic]* is served by, a prospering people.

~

In the desert years a liturgy has developed; one surmises that it much resembles a military drill. The tent is aptly named "Tabernacle of Reunion." In accord with the rite, as Moses prepares to enter the holy space, the people arise. Each family stands reverently before its dwelling, eyes fixed on the prophet.

The *shekinah* descends and envelops the Tent; parlay with great Moses is underway. And the people fall prostrate.

~

Then an astonishing statement is set down, as though matter-of-factly. And at a stroke, an entire tradition is set aside:

> Yahweh
> conversed
> with Moses,
>
> face
> to face,
>
> as
> a man
> converses
>
> with
> a
> friend. (Exod 7:11)

The genius of our author—or his effrontery! Who has heard the like? Have we not been told repeatedly with what fear and trembling Moses encounters the Categorical Imperative, the Dangerous Guardian of the Mystery, the Unutterably Transcendent?

~

Here a contrasting tradition, that of the Immanent One, is forcefully set down. Yahweh speaks:

Throughout
my house,

Moses
bears
my trust;

face-to-face

I speak
with him,

plainly

and not
in riddles.

The presence
of
the Lord

he
beholds. (Num 1:7–8)

And again, an abrupt conclusion:

Since then
no prophet
in Israel

like
Moses,

whom
the Lord
knew

face

to

face. (Deut 34:10)

~

A question haunts the mind. What is the author's view of the deity?

Complex and rich are the images. He opens a path; then with the speed of rain forest verdure, it closes behind. How are we to follow, through a thicket of seeming contradictions?

No doubt as to his intent; he means to confound us. No word or imagery is to be taken as final. There is no laying claim on his part or on ours to this deity. No metaphor suffices, no "he is unlike this" or "he is like that" can be set down by human hands in a spirit of, "Ah, now I have him!"

The tiger evades the most carefully flung net.

~

We ponder the text, astonished. A genius is at work here, and a sublime altruist as well. His spirit is detached from his own greatness. He implies, I presume no final word. I am no one's fool, no one of earth. I refuse to mark the text *finis*.

~

Closer to his method is that of the rabbis. The text grows vivacious, incandescent. It is poetry, dance, an endless mockery of puny would-be meanings, pronunciamentos, infallibilities high or low.

Nothing of these. Look down, down. See, give ear to the "widows and orphans and strangers at the gate." Their vile status, their bare-boned survival, offer the soundest clue; they are Job, legions of Jobs, those whom a morbid system has ground to anonymous paste.

The mortise of a new creation? Those plaintive voices start endless reverberations, psalms, lamentations, impetrations, curses. They will not let God off easily.

The one who thus approaches God

> retrieves the moment of Sinai. He *[sic]* is heroic, for intentionally
> or not, he puts his life in danger. He surrenders himself to the One

to whom his being and essence belong; he makes a decision, he accuses God, gives notice, confesses himself, makes a vow, accepts the yoke of His rule, pawns his soul, accepts an acquisition, and seals a covenant.[25]

—*Abraham Heschel, Polish-American rabbi and theologian*

～

Another reversal of expectation. Has the author seen what Moses saw? We stutter reading of the "face-to-face" intimacy of one among us, he of a miraculous nobility, a triumph of the human. Moses—and the "Ineffable Too Much," the "Come not Near."

This intimacy between the deity and one among us—or can it be, of two among us?

～

Perhaps we Christians see in the episode a kind of visual midrash, hinting at Things to Come:

This

we
proclaim
to you;

what was
from the beginning,

what
we have heard,

what
we have seen
with our eyes,

what
we have looked upon

and our hands
have touched—

we speak
of the Word of Life.

This Life
became visible;

we have seen
and bear witness to It,

and we proclaim
to you

the eternal Life

present
to the Father

and become visible
to us.

What
we have seen
and heard

we proclaim in turn
to you

so that you
may share

life
with us.
This fellowship
of ours

is
with the Father

and with
his Son,

Jesus
Christ. (1 John 1:1–3)

~

Verses 12–17

Shortly the tradition is welcomed into the text, tranquil and assured: friendship, sublime dialogue with the deity. *Eccolo* on our humanity, beleaguered and dismayed as we are, a crown is placed. The purport is disarming, simple, heartfelt. Moses declares in effect that a friend is one who stands with a friend, who in the rude weathers of the world walks beside.

And together, the two withstand.

~

So Moses pleads, *Walk then with us, send us no angel; it is yourself we desire in this long, baffling sojourn, whose other name is life.* He grows audacious, in the manner of an Isaiah.

If
you yourself
do not
come with us,

do not command us
to go on.

How else
will it be known

that we,
your people and I,

have found favor
with you,

except
by
your

going
with
us? (Exod 33:15–16)

~

To Christians, the passage is sublimely suggestive of another encounter,
on a far different road:

Two of the disciples
that same day
were making their way
to a village named Emmaus . . .

discussing
as they went,
all that had happened.

In the course
of their exchange,

Jesus approached
and began
to walk
along with them.

They
were restrained

from
recognizing
him . . . (Luke 24:13–16)

~

Verses 18 and following

The dialogue continues. Moses, firm, even bold, savors the love that envelops him and his people. He dares plead, *show me your glory!* (Exod 33:18).

And the response is so endearing. Ambiguous, too, in light of the earlier exchange; then, somewhere between heaven and earth, the two stood face-to-face.

(Surely no one, not even a Moses, must be allowed to presume, to think within himself: *now at long last I understand, I have this god by heart!* Such temerity is certain to be reproved, set back thunderously. In a contrary episode, the culpa will be revealed and rebuked.)

~

In any case, a contradictory text conveys a double message, a "yes, you may" and a "no, you may not." The yes-no is set before us again and again; undoubtedly it is of prime import to the author(s). We have heard the "caveat" repeatedly; to wit: no flight of language, no poetic genius, not the highest, can presume to "own" this god.

The contradictions, the tensions are all but unbearable. And they lie at the heart of the mystical experience. The god of Exodus is "seen" by Moses, only by him; that is one report. But, but . . . another, far different tradition survives. This: the god of Exodus was seen and deigned to picnic with elders of the tribe.

And the question is inevitable; was the god seen also by the author of the text?

~

As usual, the date of our final version offers a clue. In the imperial era of the great temple, rationality and logic hold sway. The best minds (the term is consonant with the iron footfall of power, in pursuit of more power)—these eminences tend toward the abstract, the quid pro quo of the mind, sound premise and sure conclusion.

Money has taken on an ominous pseudolife, a new name: Mammon. It is as though the imperial face on coins were speaking aloud, instructing their handlers as to whose pockets they would line. *Accumulation*—the buzzword.

Mammon is magnified; it has become a prime analogue of reality itself; currency value supercedes affection, compassion—those nourishing, delighting imponderables—a direct glance, an embrace, a poem, signs of freedom from appetite and domination.

~

In the era of the kings, do prophets claim mystical encounters with God? Beyond doubt they do. But the reports are ill received; the kings and their acolytes are great pragmatists, they stop their ears against words precisely aimed at excoriating their parched world. Words that would bring to naught their wicked prospering.

The prophets offer another, far different version of the imperial system. In their eyes, the superstate and its ills—greed, enslavement of the hapless and helpless, war—these are judged and found wanting: an impure darkness. A world cleft in gigantic disarray.

Reaction is sure and swift. Isaiah, Jeremiah, Ezekiel, and such as these are judged vexing and peevish. The mystics are uncontrollable. Therefore, an iron law is contrived; persecution will quench the dire forebodings they utter.

As for the priest-functionaries, their role is predictable; they follow royal suit. Covens of court prophets gain the king's ear, echo his denunciations, approve his punishments.

≈

Other times, one thinks, other strokes. The kings who preceded or were contemporary with the great prophets were granted a kind of twilit "meantime." Routine and ritual, wars and rumor of wars, were the rule. The imperial routine of divide and conquer, lay claim and loot, rolled on, for the most part unabated even under the lash of Isaiah and Jeremiah.

Earlier, such pale spirits as Nathan and Samuel came and went, seldom interfering or rebuking—or for that matter enlightening—rulers or people.

≈

Still, what a vivid memory abides (and perhaps a longing as well) for the sublime encounter—the wild embrace and burst of affection that set the desert darkness afire!

We imagine the scene; we dare place ourselves within. It goes like this—the daring, the dialogue. Moses speaks abruptly, as though his heart were bursting:

Yahweh,

let me
see

your

glory! (Exod 33:18)

And Yahweh yields; for the moment his heart, beyond custom, is worn on his sleeve. In effect, *I will pass before you, and on the moment will whisper my name to you. This I do, choosing above all—you.*

Then a second, chastened thought intrudes.

Yahweh says,

I must move with care, for no one, not even you, can see my face
and live.

See, near me,
this rock;

here
you will stand.

When my glory
passes,

I
shall set
you

in the hollow
of the rock

and cover you
with my hand,

until
I

have passed
by.

Then
I will draw

my hand
aside

so that
you
may see
my back;

but
my face

no mortal,

not even

you,

is

allowed

to

see! (Exod 33:20–23)

~

What we
have heard,

have seen
with our eyes,

what we
have looked upon

and our hands
have touched—

we speak
of the word

of
life . . . (1 John 1:1)

~

In the exodus story, the self-giving of God is rare—and when granted, overwhelming. (And in our own scripture, the gift is so—shall we say— taken for granted?)

We welcome the mysterious encounter here on the terms set, rare so rare the encounter. In the ancient testament we read and are confounded, set off-kilter. One mortal has seen God and lives. Or a number of mortals, the elders, have seen God and live.

Or, perhaps, as hinted, the author has seen God and lives.

∽

Let us be modest; the matter is serious and admits of no pride of place. We Christians are invited by our Rabbi into the circle of disciples. He would be our instructor unto life.

And our story must include its own version of the sins of Exodus. We too have reneged and defaulted and made deals and cowardly clung to safe and shoddy ways. We have hated with fervor and forgiven tardily or not at all. We continue to justify a culture that ravens about the world, seeking whom it may devour.

Such is our history. We must walk through it. The centuries, like a gauntlet of mourners with faces covered, bear witness to our crimes, our betrayals: pogroms, crusades, the *Shoah*. On and on into the woeful present. And, alas, as far as can be discerned, beyond.

∽

EXODUS 34

Moses, for his part, grows in moral stature to a truly Michelangelesque height. In time, his role as lawgiver recedes. He becomes a grand intercessor, a kind of Jesus figure before God.

Chancy too, his role! Who is to say when affairs among the people again will go badly—an outbreak of revolt, the contriving of an orgiastic idol? He must stand, uneasy between two imponderables: risk of the deific wrath and pleas for a recusant tribe.

∽

Verses 1–9

Our sense of linear time sequence—or, for that matter, our sense of standing on terra firma—these are stopped short. We are in the terrain and time of the mystics; and their time and terrain have never been clocked or mapped.

∼

We are swept along; Sinai once more, and the self-revelation of Yahweh continues apace. The moment of response arrives. Listen, Moses; listen, people! It is as though the god steps forth from the cloud of unknowing.

Tell the deity no longer how great, how good, how terrible he is. From his own lips learn who he is.

And a sea change: now he would appear in a new guise, persuasive and favorable. It is as though he grew weary of olympian heights and mists. As though in a softened moment he longs to step down and down, to join the people of the valley who, longing, gaze on high. As though he would abrogate (though he did not abrogate) the law that forbids human access. As though the deity were stirred with human yearning—to be befriended, loved, known, seen, embraced, celebrated as god-with-us. Bowing to this movement of heart, he invites Moses to his side—Moses and no other mortal.

∼

This is the solemn word: God is suffused with a passionate sense of justice, this together with a yet more passionate and finally prevailing sense of compassion. Or so it was declared on the mountain, most remarkably.

(And in the desert years, such sentiments were not often verified—we indulge in an understatement of moment—in the divine commerce with his own people).

Whatever is to be made of the confession-revelation, once more it is verified; the god is subject to a vast spectrum of moods. Presently grown reflective and benign, he grants himself—or Moses grants the god (there is rich ambiguity here)—a large store of credit:

tenderness . . .

pity . . .

slow to anger . . .

rich

in
grace
and
fidelity . . .

continuing
kindness

for

a
thousand
generations . . . (Exod 34:6)

All this, and not a whit of debit.

~

Still, a modifying record stands. More: it whirls about our heads. In accordance with that other tradition (this scroll, we are told, bears the credential of the god), other moods and tactics prevail. Tides of ire and chagrin rumble down the mountain. Liverish, petulant, guileful, vengeful—horny hands explode into the scene; these, with a coven of ghostly victims, baring their wounds in a speechless rubric of interrogation. Who, who has done this to us?

~

A shadow stands and will not dissolve. It is all the darker for the brilliant sun of self-approving mercy adduced. Second thoughts tumble after the impetuous first. *Go slow, slow!* It is as though the god were taking counsel with himself; *Let us not go too far in this matter of compassion!*

In sum, *Let us equivocate*—with a kind of conventional "on the one hand, and yet on the other."

~

We presume that the divine praise recorded here issued from the mouth of Moses. He prays as though of two minds. First, the god is expansively invited to stand before a mirror and admire what he sees: god of a thousand noble qualities.

Then, like the god, Moses undergoes a correcting second thought; *Perhaps we have given too much, let us put brakes to this racing heart of ours.*

And praise turns to a thick spittle, clogging the throat;

yet
not declaring

the guilty
guiltless,

but
punishing

children
and grandchildren

to the third
and fourth
generation

for
their
ancestors'
wickedness. (Exod 34:7)

Admiration pales; we stand appalled.

~

Verse 10

The covenant of which we have already heard much is pronounced anew. As before, it takes the form of a strict quid pro quo, a mutual binding.

One almost amended "binding" to something like "mutual servitude." At least in this sense: the god binds himself to respond in kind to the behavior of the chosen, whether good or ill.

~

We grant the holiness of the god—uncertain as to the meaning of the holiness adduced. So much of godly activity in our story has seemed positively—ungodly.

Let this be ventured, a clue riding the text. The deity is not yet free to love. To love, no matter the divagations of the chosen—golden calves, rebellions, forbidden intermarriages, darkened brows, muttering doubts and murmurations.

Gratuity is a lost art; better, an art not yet found. The deity cannot apportion largeheartedly the sweet waters of grace, free flowing, freely reconciling.

The covenant? It is a manacle; it binds him close in the Kingdom of Necessity. He must ask himself, scales in hand and weighing close, does this people merit beatitude? Then they shall have it. Or hellfire? Then, be they damned.

~

Verses 11–12

And to conclude the pact, threats and dire befallings are decreed against outsiders, those beyond the pale. The sole "crime" imputed to them, as we have seen, is prior possession of Canaan. That magical land must be seized, appropriated, given over, and this by whatever means.

And more. No gods before me!

~

Prior claims to the land fester away. And worse. Others presences, menacing, encroaching, tower on the horizon. They near, a looming nightmare—forbidden images, gods of metal, secret altars, steles. They are like specks in a perfect eye. Do these gods exist, or are they a fabrication, a monstrous mirage? Little matter, the images threaten a sovereignty that names itself absolute.

The catechesis is austere, the argument circular. Who indeed names the gods "false"? The "true" god, of course.

~

Verse 13

Then the decree: The chosen must destroy all competing altars. Every *if* and *may!* Even a hypothetical danger of pollution is accounted a horror, as though near and actual.

We consider this:

> When they wantonly worship their gods and sacrifice to them, one
> of them may invite you and you may partake of his sacrifice . . .

An invitation to genocide. And how heartily, fervently the invitation is taken up!

~

> "Pagan" means "of the land, country dweller, peasant," all of which
> my family was. It also means a person whose primary spiritual
> relationship is with nature and the earth. And this I could see
> day to day, was true not only of me but of my parents; but there
> was no way to ritually express the magical intimacy we felt with
> creation, without being accused of, and ridiculed for, indulging in
> "heathenism," that other word for paganism.
>
> And Christianity, we were informed, had fought long and
> hard to deliver us from that. In fact, millions of people were bro-
> ken, physically and spiritually, literally destroyed, for nearly two
> millennia, as the orthodox Christian Church "saved" them from
> their traditional worship of the great mystery they perceived in
> nature.[26]

—Alice Walker, American novelist and essayist

~

Verses 29–35

Henceforth, we are told, due to his communion with the almighty, the face of Moses is "horned" with light.

(In Michelangelo's *Moses*, the horns are reproduced, jutting in marble from the forehead. The legislator of the ages is seated in majesty, the tightly curled beard falls and falls, seething with life; the breast is mighty as a foothill of Sinai. Held steady and vertical, resting on the knee and supported by the vast veined hand, the famous tablets are displayed to all. It is as though the stone were doubly marmoreal, the *thou shalt* doubly underscored. The man of god has been rendered godlike. Images of the god himself are forbidden. But Moses sits there, enthroned. It is as though he not only promulgated famously the Ten Commands, but conceived them as well).

~

This remains true; Moses is no Isaiah, no Jeremiah. His soul is overpliable. He has emptied himself of will of his own; he has no argument with Yahweh:

> Moses
> did
> exactly
>
> as
> the Lord
>
> had
> commanded
> him. (Exod 40:16)

Such absolute obedience is also—deadly. It comes to this; the great subaltern will kill on command. And from on high, occasion warranting, the command is issued. Doomed are

"Amorites, Canaanites, Hittites, Perizzites, Hivetes, Jebusites" (Exod 34:11).

~

The story of conquest and pillage continues in the book of Numbers. Then likewise—you

"Moabites, Amorites, Midianites, Amalekites, Kenites, Ammonites"—and above all, you of a veritable hundred years' war, you persistent unconquerable "Philistines"!

Notes

1. Harold Bloom, "Exodus," in *Congregation: Contemporary Writers Read the Jewish Bible*, ed. David Rosenberg (San Diego: Harcourt Brace Jovanovich, 1987) 9–26.

2. David Toolan, *Facing West From California's Shores: A Jesuit's Journey into New Age Consciousness* (New York: Crossroad, 1987) 109–10.

3. "Here it is" (Italian).

4. Lev Shestov, *Athens and Jersualem*, trans. by Bernard Martin (Athens: Ohio University Press, 1966).

5. Catherine Madsen, "Notes on God's Violence," *Cross Currents* 51 (2001) 229–56; italics original.

6. Stefan George, "The Land of the Franks," in *The Works of Stefan George* (Chapel Hill: University of North Carolina Press, 1974).

7. Stanley Wolpert, *Gandhi's Passion: The Life and Legacy of Mahatma Gandhi* (New York: Oxford University Press, 2001) 6.

8. Michael E. Worsnip, "'Tribute to Fr. Michael Lapsley, SSM' May 7, 1990," in *Priest and Partisan: A South African Journey of Father Michael Lapsley*, by Michael E. Worsnip (Melbourne: Ocean, 1996) 15.

9. Joe Volk, "We Got What We Paid For," *Fellowship* (July/August 1999). Available online at: http://www.forusa.org/fellowship/jul-aug_99/wegotwhatwepaid.html (accessed 4/26/2007).

10. Elaine Scolino, "Critics Asking Clinton to Stop Advancing Missile Plan," *New York Times*, July 7, 2000.

11. Mary Condren, "To Bear Children for the Fatherland: Mothers and Militarism," *Concilium* 206 (1989) 82–90.

12. Bertolt Brecht, "The World's One Hope," in *Poems, 1913–1956*, edited by John Willett and Ralph Manheim (New York: Methuen, 1976).

13. William F. Lynch, *Images of Faith: An Exploration of the Ironic Imagination* (Notre Dame: University of Notre Dame Press, 1973) 83–84.

14. Quoted in "Commentary on the NATO bombing in Serbia and Kosovo," by Ken Sehested. See: http://www.designsbycharis.com/2003BPFNAWebsite/nato.html (accessed on April 26, 2007).

15. Cf. Michael Nagler, "Awakening Nonviolent Power, *Fellowship* (November/December 1999). Available online: http://www.forusa.org/fellowship/nov-dec_99/awakeningnvpower.html (accessed 4/26/2007).

16. Letter from Philip Berrigan.

17. Enid Nemy, "Metropolitan Diary," *The New York Times*, April 24, 2000.

18. James Alison, *Raising Abel: The Recovery of the Eschatological Imagination* (New York: Herder and Herder, 2000).

19. Annie Dillard, *For the Time Being* (New York: Knopf, 1999).

20. Gerard Manley Hopkins, "The Windhover, To Christ Our Lord," line 9.

21. Julian Borger, "'Dr. Strangeloves' Meet to Plan New Nuclear Era," *Guardian*, August 7, 2003, http://www.commondreams.org/headlines03/0807-01.htm.

22. Gerard Manley Hopkins, "Hurrahing the Harvest," lines 9–14.

23. Information from Catholic News Service on "Washington Letter" regarding the defense of School of the Americas.

24. Abraham Cohen, *Everyman's Talmud: The Major Teachings of the Rabbinic Sages* (New York: Schocken, 1995) 205.

25. From Abraham Heschel, "The Essence of Prayer."

26. Alice Walker, "The Only Reason You Want to Go to Heaven . . . ," in *Anything We Love Can Be Saved: A Writer's Activism* (New York: Ballantine, 1997) 17.